Endorsements:

In over 27 years of counseling women in abusive relationships, I have not encountered a book that so thoroughly and compassionately addresses the full spectrum of abuse—especially the covert, insidious forms that often lead to confusion, self-doubt, and emotional paralysis.

This work courageously breaks free from the conventional narratives of endurance and obligation. It is a soul-stirring call to clarity, an honest, unflinching invitation to examine one's reality. It brings structure and language to the mental chaos that abuse creates, powerfully illuminating the path to freedom from deception and control. Most importantly, it firmly guides the reader toward reclaiming their identity and security in Christ alone.

To those experiencing abuse: You will feel seen, heard, and deeply understood. Finally. You will say, "Yes! Yes, that is it! That's what I couldn't put my finger on!"

To those walking alongside them: Prepare for a perspective-shifting experience that will deepen your compassion and transform your approach to support.

-Leis Steve, Uncommon Life Ministries

Cherri Raws Freeman's insightful and informative book, *He's Clean and Sober...So Where's My Happily Ever After?*, revealed to me that addiction is often just a surface-level symptom of something far more insidious and destructive underneath. It helped me to realize that my deep sense of unworthiness and constant anxiety actually had a source. Cherri gave me the language to unravel an entire hidden subsystem of coercive control and abuse that had been flowing powerfully beneath the surface, unchecked by family members, licensed therapists, members and leaders of the church, and even by myself. With consistent truth, gentleness, impactful personal stories, scriptural clarity, and profound statements, Cherri created a space where I felt truly known and offered a clear path toward hope and healing.

    -Katie - A thankful reader

It may be unusual for a man to be endorsing a book written primarily for an audience of women! I have journeyed with Cherri for 45 years through good, bad, and ugly chapters of life. I read and scrutinized her manuscript as a male, pastor, and professor whose life bears the pain and scars of having friends and family living in the aftermath of addiction recovery and sobriety. This book shines a light on the complexity of life for a frequently forgotten or hidden audience who are bewildered and suffer in silence. It is not only insightful but also deeply convicting because it exposes the reality that, "Sobriety is step one. Healing is the real journey." Even though some of the author's truth is hard to hear, it is a masterclass in why Christians and churches must be proactive in creating space to understand, support, and walk beside those healing from many aspects of post-addition abuse.

-Dr James Ayers, PhD, Professor Emeritus, Lancaster Bible College, Capitol Seminary and Graduate School Department of Church and Ministry Leadership

My relationship with Cherri Raws Freeman spans nearly six decades. Though we had little contact for many years, we reconnected about ten years ago and quickly rediscovered a shared passion: helping women embrace their freedom in Christ. Cherri was ministering to women affected by addiction in their families, and I was working with women in the church and those facing life-controlling issues. We took an abuse advocacy course together through *Give Her Wings* and have since had many deep conversations about how the Christian community has often failed to support women in destructive and abusive relationships.

This book brings together two of Cherri's greatest passions: offering hope to women who feel forgotten after their partner's recovery, and providing practical, Christ-centered tools to help them move forward. She writes with honesty, humility, and deep compassion—for herself and for others.

Even if you're not in this situation yourself, you will gain insight, empathy, and a better understanding of how to walk alongside women who are.

-Donna

Have you ever felt like you're walking on eggshells in your marriage, waiting for the next blow-up? So many of us— strong in our faith— are silently breaking inside. Reading Cherri's book felt like someone finally saw me. With wisdom, grace, and hard-won insight, she speaks directly to women of faith who feel stuck in painful, confusing relationships. Her words bring clarity, compassion, and hope. You'll begin to see your situation for what it truly is—and discover that, even in the middle of the mess, God offers you a path toward healing and the abundant life He promises.

-Anne

This book touches on something no one talks about, especially not in the church. And yet so many of us go through it: the confusion, the loneliness, the invalidation. We don't have the words for what's happening to us, and everyone around us doesn't seem to see it. Because they've 'met Christ' or "worked on themselves,' we're supposed to believe they're healed. So then what is making me still feel this deep pain? I blamed myself through it, looked to my own shame and brokenness to explain the pain, not realizing I was in an abusive relationship.

Cherri was the first person who helped me see that just because someone recovers from addiction doesn't mean they've healed their relational patterns. Abuse can still happen. This book made me feel seen and helped me see myself. *For the first time, I felt validated, and I was able to validate myself, years after being left confused, gaslit, and convinced I was to blame.* I had so many moments reading through this book where things clicked, and words gave shape to my experience through the insight of Cherri and the experiences of others.

I found myself highlighting page zafter page. I know this will speak to other women that are unheard, unseen both by themselves and others in the midst of a confusing cloud of abuse. I pray it lands in the hands of everyone who needs it. God is using Cherri to bring truth and healing to those stuck in places that most people can't even identify. I'm excited to witness God work through Cherri's book, touching and bringing healing to many.

     -Jaylin

I thank God for using your pain and suffering through all the chaos of living with an abuser, so you can be a major help to other women suffering in silence. I too have listened to men's stories holding the mic while the wife just cringed. My husband and I have had a hard time listening to some of the men's testimony's because we saw "sobriety, but no transformation." It is so true that the man with the mic gets the praise. Thanks, Cherri, for writing this most needed book. You are a true inspiration.

     -Pat

I feel as if Cherri was living in my house during my very destructive marriage to a man who claimed to be set free from addiction and also claimed to be a pastor but was anything but. Many victims hesitate to share what is going on with their family, friends, co-workers. However, you need to listen to your gut/heart and shout from the rooftops for help as these pages come alive within you.

Cherri has reached out to us with this gift as a professional, trained through her own life's experiences, as well as her extensive education and compassion for others needing victim abuse counseling. You will recognize that it's time for additional support on your own journey within these pages, and Cherri helps you take that well-deserved first leap to an abundant life.

-Jacqui

Instead of sweeping it under the carpet or stuffing it into the closet, Cherri helps the abused deal with it and bring it into the light. Through Christ they can learn to live victoriously and be free. There is victory in Jesus. Many will learn their true identity because of this book.

-Dr. Bill Welte, Executive Director of Advancement, America's Keswick Conference Center and Addiction Recovery Ministry

In *He's Clean and Sober...So Where's My Happily Ever After?* Cherri Freeman addresses a topic I've not seen in print before but one that needs to be. When asked if she could send me a questionnaire for research, it struck me how many women I personally know who have been through similar situations. The church needs a greater understanding that sobriety is only one step in the journey to spiritual growth. I hope that Cherri's book will provide help and healing for women in post-addiction abusive relationships and encouragement to the church to provide the needed help.

-Ruth

This book is an eye opener! The trauma that women go through is written with clarity and excellence. It expounds on the truth, repentance, and healing! The book is a helpful tool for all with pliable hearts, for the church, pastors, abuser, and most importantly the person who is being abused. This book will help in guiding all to be like Christ.

-Sandra

"Cherri Raws Freeman's new book, "*He's Clean and Sober...So Where's My Happily Ever After?*" is a must read for churches and biblical counselors. Emotional abuse is little understood especially within most churches, and their ignorance of its true emotional and spiritual destructiveness is devastating to the woman who is living this nightmare. For women caught in this nightmare, this book gives them understanding, voice and hope. This book is born from her many years of her own journey of emotional and spiritual abuse. Now, God is using those years to reach out and help others caught in the nightmare and bring them safely to the other side to hope and freedom. "*He's Clean and Sober...*" needs to be in every pastor's and counselors' library."

-MaryAnn Kiernan, MA Counseling, Former Intake Coordinator America's Keswick Colony of Mercy

Cherri Raws Freeman writes another book with depth and excellence, this one about the unexpected continuation of spousal abuse after addiction recovery. It is a wealth of information, a must-read for those in abuse or who know someone who is. Cherri touches on every aspect and tackles hard truths fearlessly. She does this beautifully, with the gentleness of a compassionate counselor.

-Beth Endicott

He's Clean and Sober... is a much-needed and deeply heartfelt work, uniquely shaped by Cherri's personal journey—not only growing up at America's Keswick, but also leading a support ministry for families of those in addiction, and walking her own path through these challenges.

With both truth and compassion, Cherri sheds light on the pain, sorrow, and frustration of living with an outwardly sober spouse who continues destructive, sinful behaviors in a so-called "Christian" home. She addresses the gaslighting and misplaced shame often heaped on wives—by the ex-addict, by churches, and by well-meaning Christians—when the deep healing still needed is ignored.

-Jeanette

He's Clean and Sober... So Where's My Happily Ever After?

A GUIDE TO SEEING, NAMING, AND HEALING FROM POST-ADDICTION ABUSE

CHERRI RAWS
FREEMAN

He's Clean and Sober...So Where's My Happily Ever After

Love Them To Life Press
31A Yorktowne Pkwy
Whiting, NJ 08759
lovethemtolife@gmail.com

ISBN 978-8-218-74473-1

Cover art and formatting by Miblart.com

Printed in the United States of America

All Scripture references are from the Holy Bible, New International Version unless otherwise noted.

Dedication

For Barbara and Dorothy—two of the most beautiful souls I have ever known—who suffered torment for many years at the hands of those who had promised to love, honor, and cherish them.

When they were finally set free from their abusers, they walked forward with dignity and humor, refusing to let the past destroy their future. They loved beauty and music. They chose deep relationships and loyalty over anger and bitterness. They loved their children, grandchildren, and friends well.

My life has been richly blessed by your example and your friendship. You are my heroes.

Contents

Chapter 1:

A CALL FOR TRUTH AND HEALING

"The torrent of words came at me as a tsunami, unexpected, unstoppable, inescapable, unbearable. It had started, as tsunamis do, with a pulling back, a few moments of quiet mulling over my supposed infraction, preparing himself for the verbal attack. And then it would hit. Like a constricting snake wrapping itself around my head, the words seemed to have a life of their own, squeezing hope and peace out and replacing them with despair and questions. Had I actually done anything this time to provoke this? How can I make my apology quickly enough to avert the onslaught, all the while knowing that I hadn't done anything to cause it and was powerless to stop it. I couldn't escape to another room, as he would follow me. I couldn't get out of the house fast enough, as he would block the door or take the keys to the car. I felt as if the world were crashing in yet again. Words of condemnation and recrimination, words of shaming and guilt, words of my past failure and criticism of my children all flowed out without check or concern for the destruction he was *causing. For that was the point, after all. Destruction would keep me under control and on edge, hoping to just do enough and be perfect enough to not have to go through this again, except that was not possible. There would always be another time, and it wouldn't be far in the future. It was lurking just around the corner, waiting for him to need to get the next high of explosive anger and to keep me in my place."*

For years, this was my normal—an endless cycle of confusion, control, and emotional exhaustion. Moments like this happened so often that I stopped asking when the next one would come and started asking how I could survive them. I didn't realize then how deeply the fear, guilt, and isolation had taken hold. I only knew that I had lost my voice, my peace, and my sense of reality. And yet, like so many women in faith communities, I stayed.

Until one day, my body said what my voice could not.

"I woke up bewildered in the hospital emergency department, with no idea why I was there, when I had arrived, or why I was lying on a hospital bed when I didn't feel sick. My friend sat in the chair next to my bed, looking extremely tired and worried. A doctor came on the screen in front of me and asked me questions such as who the president was and what year it was. Usually, I was the one in the chair and X was in the hospital bed, but X was nowhere in sight, which was confusing—but also a big relief.

The day had been extremely stressful, on top of months of fatigue, pressure, and emotional uncertainty. My brain responded by going into a type of short-lived amnesia. I didn't remember the ambulance ride, CT scan, or anything that had happened for about six hours. It was as if I had been in a deep, dreamless sleep while still being awake. I couldn't create memories during that time and drove my friend crazy asking the same question over and over again every few minutes. Little did I know that it was the beginning of the end of a nightmare that had started ten years earlier.

As I lay in that hospital bed, the fog in my mind slowly began to lift—not just from the present confusion, but from the storm of the past decade that had led me there. To understand how I ended up in such a broken place, I have to go back to the beginning—back to when I first met X.

X was finishing up an internship at a rehab when I first talked with him. He had come into the program after many years of addiction to drugs, alcohol, and sex, stayed for their second-phase program, and then was offered an internship counseling and supervising the men in the first phase of rehab. He was charming, gregarious, funny, and exuded a love for Jesus. He had a powerful testimony of transformation that was engaging and encouraging. I was at a very low point in my life, having gone through a second divorce just a year prior to meeting him, and I felt as if God were very disappointed in me, at best, and done with me, at worst.

From the moment we first talked, it felt like an unstoppable force had entered my life. At the time, I believed that God had brought X to me to assist my healing and to help me know His love in a new way. After he finished his internship, he began spending nearly all day, every day at my house—probing into my past and taking up so much of my time that it became hard to think clearly. There were some red flags occasionally, but I chalked them up to his being in a process of growth after many years of destructive living. There were times that I wanted to break up with him, but then he would become incredibly loving, affirming, and overwhelming to me emotionally, and I couldn't go through with it.

Within six months, we were married—much to the dismay of my family and friends, though I didn't know about some of their concerns at the time. It felt as if I were being carried along in a rushing river, unable to get to the shore and climb out or even catch my breath.

He thought that we should go into addiction ministry—first with an organization where we trained, and later with our own non-profit. The plan was for him to work with people in addiction, and I would work with the families. On the surface, it sounded ideal. But the underlying patterns of dysfunction that had never been addressed became more and more destructive. He became seriously ill six months into our marriage and dealt with varying levels of illness throughout the years. His medical condition, combined with our shared ministry work, became the seemingly unbreakable chains that kept me tied to him.

It felt as if I were living on a rollercoaster built in a minefield. I never knew what would set him off. Once triggered, he might go on for hours—or even days—ranting at me over something I had supposedly done to hurt him. Over time, I felt increasingly isolated from my children and family. I was told that I shouldn't talk about the problems in our marriage with anyone but him. I felt as if I were walking on eggshells every moment of the day.

It seemed as if he needed my constant attention from the moment I woke up in the morning until we went to bed. Noise abuse may sound like a strange concept, but it was very real to me—it felt as if he never stopped talking, even during movies or while I was working. If I was in the shower, he would come into the bathroom and continue talking. If I asked him to stop, there would be a stretch of cold silence, followed by an outpouring of criticism—about me, my children, my past relationships—anything that could intimidate me into submission.

There were times he would quote Psalm 51 or other Scripture verses in ways that made me feel disloyal, unsubmissive, or unspiritual. These conversations left me confused and unsure of what had even started the "argument" in the first place.

After a few years, I finally opened up to several close friends and eventually to my sisters. They were incredibly supportive and helped me process the things he said so I didn't lose my grip on reality. But it was hard to find the privacy to talk. I had to be careful to erase emails and texts, as he began going through my phone and email, looking for evidence of whatever he was trying to find. My loved ones wanted me to leave long before I did, but I felt bound by the ministry, his illness, and the overwhelming guilt. How could I justify leaving someone who claimed to be dying—especially when our work and lives were so deeply intertwined?

I prayed daily that God would take one of us home in order that this would be over. I didn't want to face another divorce.

I reached out to a pastor at my church on two separate occasions to share what I was going through. He responded with concern and began meeting with X after the second conversation. I also insisted that X pursue counseling, and I began seeing a counselor myself. A ministry mentor had previously tried to help us through marriage counseling—something I now understand is not appropriate in abusive relationships. While I believe the intentions were sincere, the reality was that these efforts didn't address the core issue of abuse, and nothing truly changed.

My body began to reflect the toll of the constant stress—multiple episodes of diverticulitis eventually led to bowel resection surgery. The emotional and physical strain wore me down in every way. The deep wounds X carried from his past, combined with longstanding toxic patterns and the ongoing medical issues, created a perfect storm in our marriage that I could not weather alone.

When I ended up in the hospital—bewildered and broken—God began the work of healing that I so desperately needed. He plucked me out of a destructive situation and used the people who loved me—my children, sisters, and friends—to tell X that I would no longer be in the relationship.

My niece, thinking she'd be helping me for a few weeks, graciously took me in for nine months until the divorce was finalized and I could return to my home. Since then, God has provided every step of the way. I've entered into a new life of service through coaching and counseling women who are or have walked through difficult relationships. He continues to care for me, financially and spiritually, and often blesses

me with beautiful surprises. My family and friends are an incredible gift."

I am reminded of Psalm 40:2:
"He lifted me out of the pit of despair, out of the mud and the mire. He set my feet on solid ground and steadied me as I walked along." (NLT)

I believe in transformation. I truly do. My family legacy has been wrapped up in that concept since the 1890s when my great-grandfather found freedom from addiction and started the Colony of Mercy at America's Keswick, the oldest rehab in the country. Thousands of people have found a new life free from addiction and family dysfunction through the ministry of the Colony for men and now Barbara's Place for women.

As I watched the men of The Colony sing their theme song Victory in Jesus last night, however, I couldn't help wondering how many of them would truly find healing and how many would just get clean and sober. Through the years I have watched the metamorphosis from a life of destruction to full restoration of life in Christ in many. But there is a subset of men (and women) who retain their old relationship patterns. Yes, they are not drugging and drinking or doing any other kind of life-dominating addiction that can be seen to the outside observer, but they hold on to ways of relating that are toxic to those around them. Abusers have learned the language of transformation but refuse the process of becoming like Jesus and letting Him live His life in and through them. They wear the mask of godliness, but the fruit of the Spirit is not present in their lives. Their testimony may bring many to tears of joy, but who sees the tears of pain their wife sheds behind closed doors? Where is her miracle? The patterns of coercive control and abuse continue unabated, and yet she may feel locked in by the "testimony." Who leaves a marriage after the partner is supposedly free from addiction when she has supported him all through the process?

The purpose of this book is to bring a spotlight of truth to understand toxic patterns of relating even after someone has become sober, to show God's heart for the abused, to bring hope for life after abuse, and to encourage churches to step up to the plate to support her journey. I have walked this path myself and want you to know that there is hope. You are not alone.

While this book was written for women who are experiencing abuse and coercive control after their partner became sober, I have seen and recognize that there are abusive women who practice the same kinds of behaviors. For any man who reads this book, please know that I hear you and have great compassion for what you are experiencing. The principles are the same, no matter who is being abused, but the experience is not completely the same for men and women, so I will address the problems from a woman's perspective and pray that you will find the help you need specific to what you are going through.

The stories that are included in the book have been courageously shared by those who have been where you are. Names and identifiers have been changed to protect their privacy and safety. Some of the stories are composites of multiple women's experiences.

One of my favorite stories in the Bible is that of Hagar, the Egyptian slave of Sarai, wife of Abram. When Sarai was unable to conceive and bear an heir, she took matters into her own hands and told Abram to take her slave Hagar and use her to produce offspring (Genesis 16). This was never God's plan for Abram and Sarai, which has led to much conflict in our world. When Hagar got pregnant, Sarai abused her so much that she ran away into the wilderness. It was there that God met her and assured her of His care for her and her baby. Hagar was the first person in the Bible to give God a name: El Roi, meaning The God Who Sees. God cared for an abused, enslaved, pregnant woman. He cares for you and all that you are going through also. He sees, even when others don't or don't want to believe you.

> Psalm 34:17-19: "When his people pray for help, he listens and rescues them from their troubles. The Lord is there to rescue all who are discouraged and have given up hope. The Lord's people may suffer a lot, but he will always bring them safely through (CEV)."

A Word to Men and Pastors Reading This Book

Some readers may wonder if this book is harsh toward men or critical of the Church and its leaders. Please know that this is not the intent. I deeply believe there are good and godly men—men who stand courageously against injustice, live with integrity, and show compassion in the face of real-life struggles. I also know there are churches and pastors who faithfully walk with the wounded, supporting and serving those caught in painful and complex situations, often at great personal cost.

This book is not a blanket condemnation of men or pastors, nor an indictment of the Church as a whole. Rather, it is a focused examination of a particular kind of harm that is often misunderstood or mishandled—especially within Christian communities. Most pastors have had little or no training in recognizing coercive control or supporting victims of abuse, and many feel overwhelmed by the breadth of needs presented to them.

My hope is that you will read this with courage and curiosity—not as a critique of your heart or your calling, but as an invitation to grow in wisdom, compassion, and practical understanding. There are resources listed later in this book for training pastors and churches to be safe havens. I personally am ready to assist, encourage, empower, and teach—not to point a finger but to lend a hand.

Chapter 2:

THE MYTH OF SOBRIETY AS A CURE

"I remember thinking, "Once he's clean, everything will be okay." It felt like a promise—maybe not spoken out loud but whispered in the halls of every testimony I'd heard. Sobriety was the goal. The victory. The end of the nightmare. So, when he finally stopped using, when the lying and chaos of addiction subsided, I waited for the peace to arrive. I waited for the version of our story where healing poured in and our home filled with joy again.

But instead, I found myself staring at a man who had put down the bottle... yet still held onto control."

For many women, this is the great disillusionment. We're told that if they "just get sober," things will change. And in many ways, they do. But not always in the ways we hoped. Because sobriety is not the same as transformation—and addiction is rarely the only problem.

Addiction is, in fact, a symptom. A desperate, soul-level attempt to quiet the pain or gain control over something that feels unmanageable. It's not an excuse—but it helps explain why just removing the substance doesn't always remove the behavior.

When you grow up with a legacy like mine, where Christ-centered recovery is part of your family's DNA, you know that long-term, faith-based programs can change lives. I've seen it. I've watched the light return to eyes that were once vacant. I've heard the stories—miracles, really—of people set free. But I've also seen what happens when the story gets stuck on one chapter, when sobriety becomes the final applause, but the real work of inner change never comes.

This book is for every woman who thought she'd finally crossed the finish line... only to discover the race had just changed shape.

So, where is my fairytale ending?

This is the question that lingers in the air like a fog after the party's over, after the rehab graduation cake is eaten and the tears of joy are dried. It's the quiet cry of the wife lying in bed next to a man who is now sober but still emotionally volatile, controlling, or cold.

We were told this was the goal, right? Get him sober, and things will get better. That was the light at the end of the tunnel. It was the prize we clung to during sleepless nights and court dates and chaos. So why does it still feel so... heavy? Why does the air in the room feel like it's pressing in, like I have to hold my breath around him?

Perhaps you met and married after the big "transformation" from addiction to a sober life took place. Maybe you got drawn in to the story and believed that he indeed was your Prince Charming, only to realize that you married into a world of pain...your own personal nightmare.

Because sobriety isn't the same as healing.

No one told us that.

They didn't talk about the relational wreckage that might remain. They didn't tell us that underneath the addiction there might be pride, cruelty, deep insecurity, and entitlement. Or that sometimes sobriety just peels off the top layer, revealing someone who's more dangerous emotionally and spiritually than before.

We might hear, "You should be so grateful—he's clean now!" And yes, of course we are. But if you're honest, maybe you're also thinking, "I think I was happier when he was high." That's not a popular thing to say out loud. It sounds awful. But it's real.

Because when he was using, at least we knew what we were dealing with. There was a pattern. It made a twisted kind of sense. But now? Now he quotes parts of Scripture and weaponizes submission. Now he speaks with spiritual authority but shuts down any discussion that questions his behavior. Now the church sees him as a trophy of grace, and you feel like a doubting, bitter wife if you raise any concerns.

It's lonely. Devastatingly lonely.

This isn't the happily ever after ending you signed up for.

And if that's you, you are not crazy. You are not being overly dramatic. You are not lacking faith.

You're waking up to the truth: that sobriety, while beautiful and important, is only the *beginning*. It is not the full story of transformation. True healing is holistic—it changes not only a man's actions but his heart, his humility, the way he treats the people closest to him when no one is watching.

Testimony vs. Truth

I've heard so many testimonies in my life, when powerful stories of deliverance echoed through chapel walls and across the lake. I watched men cry on the podium, declaring they had been set free by the power of Jesus. I celebrated those stories. I still do.

But I've also watched some of those same men go home and emotionally destroy their families. I've seen the mask slip.

This is where discernment becomes so important. A testimony is only a snapshot in time. It's a moment. A testimony is not a lifetime. A testimony can be rehearsed and repeated. But fruit—the kind Jesus talked about—takes time. It grows slowly, season by season. And sometimes it reveals thorns hiding in the soil all along.

We want to believe the best. We want to hold on to hope. And I still do. But hope must be rooted in reality. In truth. Jesus said, "You will know them by their fruit" (Matthew 7:16). Not their eloquence. Not their tears. Not their polished words at the pulpit.

Is he bearing fruit?

That's the real question.

Is his life marked by love, joy, peace, patience, kindness, goodness, faithfulness, gentleness, and self-control—not just at church, but at home, behind closed doors, in the daily grind of life?

Or is he still the center of the universe, demanding your loyalty, attention, and obedience while offering very little of himself in return?

It's okay to ask these questions. It's okay to grieve the loss of the fairytale you were promised. It's okay to love someone and still set boundaries. It's okay to want more than "just sober." It's okay to hope for transformation—and also acknowledge that it hasn't happened yet.

Because here's the truth: God wants more for you than mere survival. He wants your heart to be safe. Your soul to be nourished. Your identity to be rooted in Him, not in your husband's "success story."

You are allowed to tell the truth. Even if no one else believes you yet. Even if the world claps for him and forgets about you. God has not forgotten. He sees. He knows.

He is the God who sees—El Roi, the same God who met Hagar in the wilderness when she had been used and discarded and left to fend for herself. God didn't tell her to go back and endure more abuse. He comforted her, named her, and gave her a promise for her future.

And He'll do the same for you.

When the King Baby Gets Sober

There's a term that floats around in recovery circles— "King Baby Syndrome." At first glance, it sounds kind of silly. But once you've lived with it, you know it's anything but.

A man with *King Baby Syndrome* doesn't just want attention—he demands it. He doesn't just want comfort—he demands it. He expects the world, especially his wife, to orbit around his emotional state. His moods. His needs. His pain. His preferences. And the scary part? He's not always aware he's doing it.

In addiction, this self-centeredness is masked by the chaos. We excuse it as part of the bondage. The manipulation, the gaslighting, the lying—it all gets bundled under the umbrella of "he's not himself right now."

But what happens when he *is* himself again? When he's sober—but still selfish, still controlling, still utterly unyielding in his need to be coddled and praised?

That's King Baby. And for many women, sobriety only amplifies it.

Because now, without the drug to blame, that baby king is demanding his throne in a new way. Maybe it's through spiritual superiority. Maybe it's through guilt. Maybe it's subtle—a raised eyebrow when you don't clap hard enough at his story, a quiet pout when you get support for yourself, a sigh when your needs don't line up with his timeline.

Sometimes it's overt—like a rebuke wrapped in Scripture. "You're supposed to submit." "You're supposed to forgive."

"You're not being a helpmeet." All while his own emotional maturity is still stunted, stuck in toddler-mode, and your soul is quietly suffocating under the weight of all his unhealed baggage.

I know this might be hard to read. But someone has to say it: sobriety does not crown him king. It's not the final miracle. It's not the ribbon at the end of the race.

Sobriety is step one.

Healing is the real journey. And *mutual* healing—the kind that values your heart also—is the only kind worth building a future on.

The Big Testimony Trap

In many churches, there's a kind of reverence around "the testimony." That moment when someone stands up, microphone in hand, and tells the dramatic story of how God rescued them from the pit. We love those stories. We celebrate them. We *should*.

But I've seen what happens when a woman tries to tell her side of the same story—and the church isn't ready to hear it.

Because while he's up front declaring victory, she's still bleeding out in the pew.

While the audience is clapping, she's quietly unraveling, questioning her own reality, wondering if she's the crazy one. Wondering what the next offense will be that will trigger a tirade and why she can't just do everything "right."

Because if he's healed, why does she still feel so broken?

If God rescued him, why is she still drowning?

Here's the danger: when a testimony becomes a *performance*, it leaves no room for process. It leaves no room for accountability. It leaves no room for the wives, the children, the families still picking up the pieces behind the scenes.

And when that testimony becomes the man's *identity*, he will protect it at all costs—even if it means minimizing, denying, or rewriting history.

The "Big Testimony" can become a trap, not just for him, but for *you*—because any pain you express now sounds like you're raining on God's parade.

There are women in churches who say, "When I tried to talk about the emotional abuse, they said I was bitter. That I was trying to destroy his reputation. That I should be grateful God set him free."

I want to say to every single one of those women: *You are not crazy. You are not bitter. You are telling the truth.*

There's room in the Kingdom for your story, too.

You matter just as much as the man with the mic. Your healing matters just as much as his sobriety. Your wounds are not less valid just because he has a "testimony."

And if you are still being harmed—emotionally, verbally, spiritually—then that is not healing. That is not the Gospel.

That is a golden calf wearing a Christian t-shirt.

You are allowed to name what's happening. You are allowed to step out of denial. You are allowed to say, "This is not okay," even when the world says, "But he's sober now."

Sobriety is beautiful.

But it is not the same as repentance.

And God calls us to truth. To justice. To peace. Not to pretend. Not to suffer silently so someone else can keep their platform.

You don't have to protect his image at the cost of your soul. You can step into the light too.

The Truth Will Set You Free

You may be reading this chapter and feeling like you've just had a bucket of cold water thrown over you. Maybe you're finally seeing things for what they are. Maybe you're staring at the wreckage of a life you thought was on the mend, only to realize it's still crumbling underneath the weight of toxic patterns. Maybe you're questioning your own role in all of this—wondering if you're just being too hard, too bitter, too unrealistic. Maybe you met and married someone who promised you the world, only to recognize that the old patterns of his previous life are still there, just dressed up in cleaner, fancier clothes.

But here's the truth: You are not crazy. You are not the villain in someone else's fairytale. You are *not* responsible for someone else's addiction, their recovery, or their refusal to truly change. You are not called to live in a toxic relationship in the name of "grace" or "submission." God has not called you to a life of endless pain, manipulation, and emotional death.

You are allowed to set boundaries. You are allowed to demand accountability. You are allowed to heal. And your healing is just as important as anyone else's.

Maybe you've been clinging to the hope that sobriety would fix everything. But now you know that sobriety is just the beginning. It's a step, not a finish line. And for those of us in relationship with someone who is sober but still emotionally abusive, the journey of healing is just as much about *us* as it is about them.

This chapter isn't meant to tear down anyone's recovery story or undermine the power of God's transformative work. Sobriety *is* a miracle. But we must not mistake that miracle for the total transformation God wants to bring about in each of us—body, soul, and spirit. And we must not allow ourselves to remain in destructive relationships that are rooted in control, manipulation, or abuse under the guise of grace.

It's okay to say, "This is not enough." It's okay to seek out help and healing for yourself, not just for your spouse. It's okay to find your voice again, even when others don't understand it. It is ok to realize that you were lured into the lion's den by what you thought were the purrs of a kitty cat.

Moving Forward: The Path to Real Healing

Healing begins when we acknowledge what is true. We must see our stories clearly, without the rose-colored glasses of "big testimonies" or "spirituality" that gloss over deep wounds. God does not want us to live in denial; He wants us to live in *freedom*. True freedom comes when we stop pretending and start facing the truth.

If you're in a relationship where sobriety has not led to the change you hoped for, let this chapter be a wake-up call. You do not have to remain in this unhealthy dynamic. There is a path forward—a path to healing, to wholeness, and to freedom.

It may be a hard road. It may require counseling, setting boundaries, separating for a season, or even walking away entirely. But one thing I know for sure: you were not made to be a victim. You were made to be a *warrior* for your own soul, for your peace, for your well-being.

And as you embark on that journey, remember that God is not finished with you. He sees you. He hears you. And He is waiting to guide you through the darkness into His light.

In the chapters to come, we'll unpack these ideas more deeply, especially the importance of understanding trauma bonding, the truth about abusive patterns, and how to find spiritual and emotional healing that goes beyond sobriety.

Remember: You are not alone in this.

Cling tightly to the mane of the Lion of Judah.

Your healing *matters*.

And the story isn't over yet.

Chapter 2 Discussion Questions

1. When you first hoped for (or experienced) your partner's sobriety, what did you imagine life would feel like six months later? In what ways did reality match—or shatter—those expectations?

2. Read Matthew 7:16 and Galatians 5:22–23. Looking at your relationship today, where do you see genuine fruit of the Spirit? Where is it notably absent?

3. List three behaviors that still center your spouse's comfort above everyone else's well-being. How have you been trained to adapt or minimize those behaviors?

4. Think of a time the church celebrated your partner's story. How did that public narrative affect your private reality and your ability to ask for help?

5. Which sentence or paragraph in this chapter felt like a "bucket of cold water" moment for you? What truth did it name that you've struggled to articulate?

6. Based on what you've realized, what is one boundary, conversation, or act of self-care you can commit to this week to move toward holistic healing—for you?

Chapter 3:

THE INTERSECTION OF BODY, SOUL, AND SPIRIT IN ADDICTION AND ABUSE

Emily's Story:

When Emily walked into the room, she felt an overwhelming sense of shame. It wasn't because of what others might think of her—she had long since grown accustomed to hiding behind a mask of perfection. No, the shame she carried was deeper. It was an ache in her soul, a realization that no matter how hard she tried to make things right, she could never seem to escape the cycle she found herself trapped in.

Her marriage to Matt had started out like a dream. He had overcome his addiction prior to meeting her and seemed to love Jesus so much. He was charming, attentive, and seemed to care deeply about her well-being. But as time went on, things began to change. Matt's temper flared more easily. He would come home late from work and be distant, even cold. What had once been a warm, loving relationship had slowly deteriorated into something unrecognizable. Emily had learned to walk on eggshells, never quite sure when Matt would snap or when his words would cut her like a knife.

And yet, in the midst of it all, Matt would have moments of tenderness—his apologies, his promises to change, and the occasional "I love you" that seemed to erase all the hurt. The highs and lows left Emily dizzy, unsure of what was real anymore.

The turning point came one night when Emily confronted Matt about the emotional neglect, about the way his anger seemed to come out of nowhere. His response wasn't what she expected. It wasn't a promise to work on things or an acknowledgment of his fault. Instead, Matt's eyes grew dark, and he accused her of being the problem. He told her that he had accepted Christ and was living a new life. She, on the other hand, was just holding on to her past. She needed to forgive and forget. She needed to trust him more.

In that moment, Emily realized something that shook her to the core: Matt's faith—if it was even real—wasn't transforming his life in the ways that mattered most. He still controlled, still manipulated, still blamed others for his shortcomings. She wondered how many times he had spoken the words of Scripture, teaching others about grace and forgiveness, while behind closed doors, he was continuing to break her down.

Emily's story is not unique. There are many who, like Matt, may have experienced the life-changing power of salvation in their spirits but have not allowed it to reach their souls or their bodies. They may wear the mask of a transformed person, but inside, they are still broken—still clinging to their old patterns of control, manipulation, and self-sufficiency. They may not be drinking or doing drugs anymore but in reality, those habits are the only things that have changed. Their faith has not informed their life.

In this chapter, we will explore the intersection of body, soul, and spirit, and how healing from addiction and abuse must address each of these areas. We will also look at how the root of toxic relational patterns often runs deeper than addiction itself—into the woundedness of the soul and the failure to allow the Spirit of God to bring true transformation to every aspect of a person's being.

The Body: The Physical Manifestation of Wounds

The body is often where we see the most visible consequences of addiction and abuse. Whether it's through substance abuse, unhealthy coping mechanisms, or the toll of chronic stress and fear, our physical bodies bear the scars of our inner turmoil. Addiction is a physical phenomenon that involves our bodies' craving and dependence on a substance or behavior. These cravings are not only chemical but emotional, tied to the deep need for comfort or escape from pain. Yet, as much as addiction has a physical component, the body is also where the impact of relational trauma shows up. Chronic stress, tension, and the physiological impact of abuse—whether emotional, verbal, or physical—can manifest in ways that may seem disconnected from the soul but are deeply intertwined.

Red Flag Symptoms of Chronic Stress: headaches, jaw tension, insomnia, gastrointestinal issues, autoimmune flare-ups, frequent colds.

The body, in many ways, holds the tension between sin and redemption. The damage done by addiction and abuse can create a physical brokenness that no amount of willpower can heal. However, the process of transformation takes place in the body as well. Healing the body—through rest, nutrition, and exercise—can be a first step toward healing the soul. In Romans 12:1, Paul urges believers to offer their bodies as living sacrifices to God, holy and pleasing to Him. This involves both recognizing our bodily limitations and honoring the body as part of God's good creation. This does not mean that physical healing is the ultimate goal, but it is a crucial component of the healing process.

The Soul: The Core of Our Emotional and Relational Struggles

The soul, encompassing the mind, will, and emotions, is where the most significant battle lies in the context of addiction and abuse. Our minds are shaped by our thoughts, our emotions by our feelings, and our will by our desires. When we've been wounded by addiction or abusive relationships, our soul becomes a battleground. Traumatic experiences, whether from addiction itself or from relational abuse, often distort our emotional reactions, our ability to think clearly, and our capacity to make healthy choices.

Dr. Gabor Maté's insights into the role of trauma in addiction shed light on how deeply the soul is affected when he said, "Not all traumatized people become addicted, but all addicted people were traumatized."[i]

Early trauma can alter the way our brain functions, leading to dysfunctional emotional responses and unhealthy coping mechanisms. In many cases, the addicted person's soul is still entangled in the false beliefs, lies, and fears developed in response to their trauma. They may act out of these wounds in relational patterns that perpetuate abuse and control.

Healing the soul, then, is not simply about changing our behavior. It involves deep, painful work in addressing the root causes of emotional scars. As Dr. Marcus Warner of Deeper Walk International describes, we must identify the wounds we have received, the lies we believe, and the vows we make that lock us into destructive patterns or strongholds. Only then can we begin to reframe our identities and understand who we truly are in Christ.[ii] For example:

- **Wound**: Betrayed by a parent
- **Lie**: I'm not worth protecting
- **Vow**: I will never depend on anyone again
- **Stronghold**: Numbing the pain with some sort of destructive behavior, unhealthy pattern of relationships, or coping mechanisms that are unhelpful.

Healing the soul involves exposing these strongholds and replacing them with truth. Romans 12:2 instructs: "Do not be conformed to this world but be transformed by the renewal of your mind." This renewal comes through the truth of God's Word, the influence of the Holy Spirit, and the support of a healthy community. Without this, we may find ourselves stuck in unhealthy relational patterns, perpetuating cycles of abuse or addiction.

The Spirit: The New Creation and the Source of True Freedom

The spirit is where true transformation begins. When someone comes to Christ, they are made new in their spirit; they are born again (John 3:3-8). This transformation is immediate but must be worked out in the soul and body over time.

The Spirit of God in a believer's life is the power that allows them to break free from the cycles of addiction, manipulation, and abuse. It is the Holy Spirit who empowers us to walk in newness of life and equips us with the fruit of the Spirit to exhibit love, peace, patience, and self-control (Galatians 5:22-23).

But the presence of the Spirit doesn't automatically eliminate destructive behavior. Many people who claim to follow Jesus still walk "in the flesh"—living on their own terms rather than by the Spirit. This is why many people who claim to be followers of Jesus still struggle with abusive tendencies, selfishness, and manipulation. It is not that they don't have a new spirit; it's that the spirit has not yet been allowed to fully transform the soul and the body. Sanctification is the process of yielding to God in every area of life and growing into Christlikeness in a lifelong journey. It is living in union with Jesus, day by day, moment by moment.

True spiritual transformation becomes visible when:

  - There is genuine remorse, not just apology.
  - A person invites accountability rather than avoids it.
  - There is openness to feedback and correction.
  - There is consistent, humble pursuit of healing over time.

The Danger of Unhealed Wounds:
Toxic Relational Patterns

When addiction and abuse patterns go unhealed, they permeate every relationship, from family to friendships, and especially intimate partner dynamics. As we can see, those who claim spiritual transformation may appear to be "masking" the deeper issue. They may talk the talk but fail to walk the walk, especially in their most intimate relationships. The true test of transformation lies not in outward behavior or public display of faith but in the deeper transformation of the soul.

Ask yourself the following: does the person exhibit the fruit of the Spirit? Do they admit when they are wrong? Do they use Scripture to shame or silence? Are they truly walking in love, gentleness, and self-control? Are they capable of deep, vulnerable connection, or do they still use manipulation and control?

It is essential for those in abusive relationships to understand that spiritual transformation is not just about attending church or reading Scripture. Spiritual maturity shows up in how someone loves, how they listen, and how they respond when challenged. When we see ongoing patterns of control, dismissal, or entitlement, it's a sign that soul work remains undone. It's about allowing the truth of who we are in Christ to change the way we relate to others. And this takes time, healing, and the willingness to face the painful realities of our wounds. Unfortunately, it does not always happen.

If you're in a relationship with someone whose healing has stopped at the surface, it's not unspiritual to recognize it. In fact, it's wise. Jesus told us to judge a tree by its fruit (Matthew 7:16).

Conclusion: Moving Toward Healing and Restoration

As we close this chapter, we've seen how addiction and abuse affect every part of a person—the body, the soul, and the spirit—and how true healing must reach into each of these areas. But for many women like Emily who are living in relationships marked by control, manipulation, and emotional harm, healing is not just about personal restoration. It's about recognizing the abusive dynamics they are trapped in and understanding how these patterns persist even after the surface-level change of sobriety or spiritual talk.

True healing is not about managing someone else's change. It's about seeking your own. That journey may include counseling, setting boundaries, or speaking the truth in love. It may involve grieving, distancing. or even leaving. Whatever the path, you are not alone. There is hope.

In the next chapter, we will turn directly to the hard and often hidden topic of abuse and coercive control: what it looks like, why it is so damaging, and how women of faith can begin to name what's happening and take steps toward freedom.

Chapter 3 Discussion Questions

1. **Mirror Check**

   Emily describes feeling "dizzy, unsure of what was real." Think of a recent interaction where you felt similarly disoriented. What triggered that feeling— words, tone, or hidden threat?

2. **Body Signals**

   List two physical symptoms you notice when stress in your relationship spikes. What might your body be telling you that your mind has learned to dismiss?

3. **Wounds–Lies–Vows–Strongholds**

   Identify one wound, one lie, and one vow you've internalized. How have these shaped your relational patterns? What strongholds can you identify in your own life?

4. **Soul Renewal**

   Romans 12:2 speaks of renewing the mind. What biblical truth most directly counters the lie you identified above?

5. **Spirit Audit**

   Look at Galatians 5:22-23. Which part of the fruit of the Spirit is missing in your relationship dynamic? How does naming that absence help clarify your next step?

6. **Next Brave Step**

   Choose one area—body, soul, or spirit—and set a single, attainable goal for the coming week. What will support your follow-through?

Chapter 4:

COERCIVE CONTROL—THE HIDDEN ABUSE

"Stop waiting for him to be the man he tricked you into believing he was in the beginning."

— Helena Knowlton

Story: "Kari's Quiet Undoing"

Kari didn't know the exact moment she lost herself.

It hadn't happened all at once. There were no slammed doors, no bruises to explain. Just little things. He started insisting on knowing where she was at all times—"just to be safe." Then came the concerns about her friends. "They don't share our values," he'd say. "They're bad influences." Eventually, she stopped meeting them for coffee.

When they first met, he had been open about his past—years of addiction to alcohol, drugs, and pornography. But he also had a dramatic testimony of deliverance and healing. He spoke boldly at church about how God had changed his life. Kari believed him. Everyone did. She thought she was marrying a miracle.

But as time passed, something felt off. He became controlling, possessive. Hyper-spiritual when it suited him. He began reviewing her texts, her emails, her online purchases. He said it was about trust—but he never seemed to trust her. And when she cried, he said she was being dramatic. Ungrateful. Unsubmissive.

She tried to bring it up at small group once, careful to speak in generalities. His smile tightened beside her. Later that night, he quoted Proverbs about a quarrelsome wife and suggested she pray about her attitude. He said she was damaging his testimony.

Kari prayed harder.

He wouldn't let her take the kids to her old church anymore, saying the teaching was "watered down." He encouraged her to stop working so she could focus on the home—on him. "It's biblical," he reminded her.

She didn't realize she'd stopped making decisions for herself until the day she stood in the grocery store aisle, paralyzed over whether to buy the brand of cereal he didn't like. Her heart pounded like a trapped animal. Her hands shook. That was when she heard it—her own voice, quietly whispering: Who have I become?

She had always thought abuse would be loud. Violent. Obvious. She had no idea it could be so quiet, so devout, so praised by the people around her.

Kari's story isn't rare. In fact, it's a devastatingly familiar reality for many Christian women—where coercive control hides in plain sight, cloaked in Scripture, sincerity, and silence.

Introduction: When Abuse Hides in Plain Sight

For many women, abuse doesn't begin with a bruise. It begins with a shift. A quiet erasure of voice. A weight in the chest that doesn't go away. A growing sense that no matter how carefully they walk, they are always stepping on a landmine.

It doesn't always look like the world imagines abuse to look. It rarely starts with fists or threats. Sometimes, it starts with a Bible verse. A sermon. A raised eyebrow. A chilling silence. A look that says: *You're mine to control.*

And for those in Christian communities, the confusion cuts even deeper. How can something that feels so wrong come wrapped in the language of love, leadership, and spiritual authority? How do you explain the ache in your soul when your partner never lays a hand on you—but controls every part of your world? How do you name what's happening when everyone around you calls it "headship," "submission," or "just part of marriage"?

This is coercive control. It is abuse, even when no one else can see it.

It is the slow suffocation of a woman's personhood. It is a pattern of behaviors designed to dominate, dismantle, and disorient—until she questions her own sanity, her own worth, and even her own faith.

In the pages that follow, we will name it plainly. Not to stir up division or place blame—but to bring clarity, language, and light to what has long been hidden in the shadows. You are not imagining things. You are not alone. And you are not crazy.

God is not the author of abuse, even if someone uses His name to justify it.

Let's begin by understanding what coercive control really is.

What Is Coercive Control?

Coercive control is a strategic pattern of behavior used to dominate, manipulate, intimidate, and limit a partner's freedom. Unlike single incidents of abuse, coercive control is more comprehensive and insidious, governing the whole of a person's life. The goal is not just to win arguments or get one's way, but to entrap and subjugate, to make the victim doubt her own power, voice, and right to choose.

This form of abuse can be subtle—and often is. It may include surveillance, isolation, spiritual manipulation, economic control, and ongoing threats. Over time, it wears down a person's mental and emotional health, distorts her sense of reality, and conditions her to feel helpless. She may not even recognize she is being abused—only that she feels smaller, silenced, and somehow always in the wrong.

Dr. Debra Wingfield, a respected advocate and expert in coercive control, puts it this way:

"Abusers exert coercive control verbally, emotionally, and mentally through gestures, degradation, mind games, humiliation, restriction, and manipulation."[iii]

She goes on to say that coercive control doesn't require physical force. Its power lies in a calculated web of tactics designed to restrict nearly every area of a victim's life—from movement and behavior to parenting, intimacy, and connection. She goes on to say the following:

"Coercive control uses multiple tactics designed to:

- Restrict movements
- Restrict behaviors
- Restrict thoughts
- Restrict feelings
- Restrict actions
- Restrict economics
- Restrict parenting
- Restrict intimacy
- Restrict relationships
- Restrict connections
- Restrict autonomy
- Restrict access
- Restrict self-control"[iv]

These methods are not random. They are part of a calculated strategy, often masked as "concern," "leadership," or "godly headship." But their effect is to dismantle a woman's autonomy and keep her trapped under the guise of love, faith, or marital obligation.

How Coercive Control Works

Coercive controllers often employ a deliberate set of tactics to break down their partner's resistance and enforce submission. These include the following, according to Dr.Wingfield:

- Intimidation
- Isolation
- Economic or financial control
- Threats
- Using children
- Emotional abuse
- Using male privilege
- Minimizing, denying, and blaming
- Control tactics
- Spiritual abuse
- Non-physical sexual abuse
- Physical abuse
- Physical sexual abuse[v]

These are not occasional lapses in anger. They are tools of domination used to destabilize, confuse, and control.

One of the clearest frameworks for understanding coercive control is Biderman's Chart of Coercion, originally developed by Amnesty International in 1994 to describe methods used against prisoners of war. Survivors of domestic abuse quickly recognized these same tactics in their homes—not with guards or interrogators, but with spouses who claimed to love them

Biderman's Chart of Coercion:

1. **Isolation:** Cutting off access to friends, family, support systems—often framed as protection or spiritual leadership.
2. **Monopolization of Perception:** Keeping the victim focused entirely on the abuser's needs, emotions, and demands—and creating confusion between kindness and cruelty.
3. **Humiliation and Degradation:** Through insults, restrictions on hygiene or privacy, or demeaning punishments.
4. **Exhaustion:** Depriving sleep, rest, or food, or creating constant emotional stress to wear down resistance.
5. **Threats:** Threats of harm, abandonment, spiritual condemnation, or suicide, with the blame placed on the victim.
6. **Occasional Indulgences:** Periods of kindness or empty promises ("future faking") to keep the victim hopeful and compliant.
7. **Demonstrating Omnipotence:** Showing force, breaking things, or making sure the victim knows she cannot "win."
8. **Enforcing Trivial Demands:** Constantly changing rules and expectations so the victim is always uncertain and always wrong.

Coercive Control in a Christian, Faith-Based Relationship

To understand how coercive control operates in a faith setting, let's look at an example.

Helen and James:

Helen, a devout Christian, married James, a man with a past addiction who was now a respected leader in their church. In public, he shared his testimony and was admired. But behind closed doors, James became increasingly controlling—using spiritual authority as his justification.

Tactics He Used:

- **Spiritual Manipulation:** Selectively quoting Ephesians 5:22 while ignoring mutual submission and love. Accusing Helen of rebellion or sin when she expressed disagreement or concern.
- **Isolation:** Discouraging outside friendships and Bible studies not led by him. Monitoring phone use and social media.
- **Emotional and Psychological Abuse:** Gaslighting her concerns, comparing her to "Proverbs 31," and belittling her spiritual life.

- **Financial Control:** Refusing to let her work, giving her a small allowance to cover the household expenses with strict oversight, and excluding her from family financial decisions.
- **Sexual Coercion:** Demanding sex using misapplied Scripture. Ignoring illness or fatigue. Framing her refusal as disobedience to God.
- **Threats and Intimidation:** Warning her that leaving would mean spiritual judgment, loss of community, or abandonment by God.

Impact on Helen:

She began to question her worth, her faith, and even her sanity. Isolated, spiritually confused, and emotionally drained, she stayed—not out of love, but out of fear.

Why This Thrives in Church Settings

Coercive control is especially dangerous in patriarchal or legalistic church environments. When spiritual authority is used to justify hierarchy, and submission is emphasized without accountability, abuse can flourish, unchecked and even encouraged.

This kind of control isn't limited to a single denomination or theological view. But in faith settings where the husband's "headship" is treated as unquestionable, and a wife's submission is taught as spiritual duty, victims are often blamed for their own suffering or told they are failing to be "godly wives."

Legal Recognition and Advocacy

In recent years, the legal system has started catching up. Several U.S. states and the United Kingdom now recognize coercive control as a form of domestic abuse and, in some jurisdictions, a criminal offense.

Advocates such as Dr. Debra Wingfield and organizations like Called to Peace Ministries have played key roles in raising awareness and shaping laws to protect victims.

Coercive control is not "just a difficult marriage." It's not something to be solved in counseling or prayer alone. It is a deeply destructive pattern that requires truth, boundaries, and, often, outside intervention.

Abuse and Coercive Control: A Wider Lens

Coercive control is the foundation beneath most other forms of abuse. Whether physical, emotional, financial, or sexual, the aim is the same: to dominate, silence, and isolate.

In the next chapter, we'll take a closer look at these various types of abuse—how they appear, how they affect the victim, and how they are often overlooked or minimized in Christian homes and churches.

Chapter 4 Discussion Questions

1. In what ways have you experienced or witnessed coercive control that didn't involve physical violence but still left deep wounds?
2. Biderman's Chart lists tactics like isolation and exhaustion. Which one resonates most with your experience or makes you pause?
3. In the example of Helen and James, which tactic felt most familiar? How did it make you feel to see it named?
4. Has spiritual language ever been used against you to silence, shame, or manipulate? How did that affect your view of God?
5. What is one truth from Scripture that affirms your worth and counters the control you've experienced?
6. If you suspect you're experiencing coercive control, what's one small but brave step you can take to move toward safety or clarity?

Chapter 5:

THE MANY FACES OF ABUSE

What Is Abuse?

Abuse is not always obvious. It doesn't always come with bruises, screaming, or broken furniture. Sometimes it comes with silence or with pressure. With Scripture quoted out of context. With confusion and pain that has no name.

Abuse is defined as:

> *"Any action that intentionally harms or injures another person."*
>
> — *Gale Encyclopedia of Medicine*

At its core, any type of abuse is a misuse of power—one person exerting control over another through fear, punishment, manipulation, or intimidation.

It can be visible or invisible. It may be physical, emotional, sexual, financial, or spiritual. But all forms of abuse have the same underlying goal: **to dominate and silence.**

This chapter names those forms clearly—not to overwhelm, but to help you recognize what may have been happening in your life, often unnoticed, for years.

Physical Abuse

Physical abuse includes any use of physical force intended to control, punish, intimidate, or harm. It may be overt or covert (carefully hidden). Many abusers target areas of the body that don't easily show bruises.

Red-flag behaviors:

- Hitting, punching, kicking, biting, choking, or slapping.
- Using objects (belts, cords, fists) to inflict pain.
- Blocking doorways or taking keys to prevent someone from leaving (unlawful restraint).
- Throwing objects, punching walls—even if it doesn't hit the victim.
- Depriving someone of food, water, warmth, clothing, rest, or access to a bathroom.
- Driving erratically to scare the victim into doing what he wants. Road rage and intimidation. Following the

victim in a car and driving in a threatening way. Using the car as a weapon.

Rachel's Story: Weaponized Wheels

For years, Rachel thought the worst of the abuse was behind them. Her husband, Matt, had gotten clean. He was no longer disappearing on drug binges or screaming through the house at 2 a.m. He had a job now. They went to church. From the outside, everything looked better.

But in private, Matt still controlled everything—especially when he was behind the wheel.

It started subtly. If Rachel asked to stop for groceries, he'd say no or pass the exit without a word. If she asked where they were going, he'd snap, "You don't need to know. Just sit there."

Then came the erratic driving.

He'd accelerate suddenly on the highway during arguments, swerving in and out of traffic while she begged him to slow down. He once veered off the road just to prove a point—his hands off the wheel, eyes locked on her in a chilling stare. Rachel sat frozen, heart pounding, knowing better than to scream. That would only make him angrier.

Matt liked to call it "just blowing off steam." But Rachel began to realize: the car was his stage. It was the one place she was completely trapped, where he had all the power and she had none. He knew it.

Sometimes he'd brake hard at intersections just to make her flinch. Other times, he'd speed up while tailgating someone, then scream out the window and slam the horn until Rachel cried. He'd smile afterward and say, "You're so sensitive. It's not like I hit you."

But the car was never safe.

Eventually, when Rachel started going to counseling on her own, Matt began following her. She'd see his truck in her rearview mirror, parked across from the church office or slowly rolling by as she walked to her car. He never got out. He didn't need to. She got the message.

It wasn't about transportation anymore. It was about control, fear, and domination. Just because he wasn't striking her with his fists didn't mean she wasn't being terrorized.

Matt used a two-ton machine as an extension of his temper—a vehicle not just for movement, but for threat. And for Rachel, every drive became a silent question: Will I survive this ride?

Legal Note: When Driving Becomes a Weapon

Using a vehicle to intimidate, control, or terrify someone can cross the line into **criminal behavior**—even if no physical contact occurs. In many jurisdictions, this type of behavior may fall under:

- Reckless endangerment.
- Assault (by means likely to cause harm).
- Stalking or harassment, if the abuser follows or surveils the victim using a vehicle.

- Coercive control, where laws exist to prosecute patterns of intimidation and domination.

Some states and countries are beginning to recognize **non-physical forms of abuse**—like weaponized driving—as legitimate forms of domestic violence. These behaviors may also be used as evidence in custody cases, protective order filings, or police reports, especially if they create a pattern of fear or danger.

If you're documenting abuse, it's important to **note the date, time, and details** of incidents like erratic or threatening driving, even if it didn't result in a crash. Just because it doesn't leave bruises doesn't mean it isn't violence.

Evie's Story: Married to His Recovery, Bruised by His Hands

I didn't think it was abuse. Not at first.

He was clean. Sober for two years. Everyone at church said how proud they were of him. He gave his testimony on Sunday mornings—how God had delivered him from alcohol and drugs. People clapped. Some cried. I sat in the front row, trying to keep smiling.

They didn't see what happened when we got home.

He never left marks on my face. He was smarter than that. It was pushing. Grabbing. Shoving me against the wall when I questioned him. Yanking the steering wheel when I "disrespected him" while driving. Slamming the door inches from my head. One night, he picked up a mug and threw it so hard it shattered against the cupboard behind me.

When I told a friend, she said, "Well... at least he's not drinking anymore. That counts for something."

But did it?

His fists didn't need alcohol to fly into the drywall. His rage didn't need drugs to erupt when dinner wasn't ready, or the baby wouldn't stop crying. He wasn't drunk when he pinned me to the bed and told me I made him act this way. He wasn't high when he held my wrists and hissed through gritted teeth that if I ever disrespected him again, I'd be sorry.

And still, he prayed before meals. Still, he led devotions. Still, he told everyone he was a changed man.

And I felt like I was the only one still bleeding.

It took me years to say the word "abuse." For a long time, I just called it "conflict" or "anger issues." But it wasn't mutual. It wasn't normal. And it wasn't safe.

The turning point came the night he pushed me, hard, while I was holding our toddler. I fell back into the couch and caught myself—but I felt something in me snap. Not physically. Spiritually. Emotionally. I couldn't explain it, but I knew: This is not what God meant by headship. This is not love.

I didn't leave that night. But I made a plan. I reached out to a domestic violence hotline. I started documenting. I spoke to a trauma-informed counselor at a local church, one who didn't minimize or shame me. She called what I described "coercive control with physical violence." She said the words I hadn't been able to speak: You are not crazy. You are not weak. And this is not your fault.

Eventually, I left. It was terrifying. But God met me in the wilderness. In the quiet. In the shaking moments of starting over. And He never looked away.

I still flinch sometimes when someone moves too fast. But I don't live in fear anymore. I live in peace.

Physical abuse is not just about bruises or broken bones—it's about the message that your safety, dignity, and autonomy don't matter. Many women in Christian marriages struggle to reconcile the violence with the testimony, the prayers with the pain. But Scripture never excuses harm in the name of headship, nor does sobriety erase accountability. If you are being physically hurt, pushed, or threatened, even without visible injuries, it is not your fault. You deserve safety. God does not ask His daughters to endure violence to preserve someone else's image of redemption. He sees, He cares—and He calls harm what it is.

Emotional and Verbal Abuse

Verbal abuse uses words to attack, belittle, and control. It may be loud and cruel or quiet and cutting. Emotional abuse uses these words—and other tactics—to destroy a person's inner world and sense of self.

Verbal abuse may include:

- Yelling, name-calling, criticism.
- Sexual slurs or degrading comments.

- Mockery, threats, or humiliation.
- Judging one's intelligence, parenting, or spirituality.

Emotional abuse may include:

- Using children as weapons.
- Manipulating with guilt, shame, or silence.
- Blaming the victim for everything wrong in the relationship.
- Withholding affection as punishment.
- Gaslighting - Gaslighting is a form of psychological manipulation where someone causes you to doubt your own reality—your memories, your feelings, or even your sanity. It's more than just lying; **it's a strategic twisting of truth designed to confuse, destabilize, and control.**

You might bring up something hurtful your partner said, only to hear, "*That never happened,*" or "*You're too sensitive,*" or "*You always make things worse than they are.*" Over time, you may begin to second-guess yourself: *Maybe I misunderstood. Maybe it really is my fault. Maybe I am crazy.*

Gaslighting erodes your ability to trust your own instincts. It isolates you not just from others—but from your own God-given discernment. This is why gaslighting is so spiritually dangerous: it disconnects you from the truth, and from the voice of the Holy Spirit who speaks through conviction, not confusion.

The enemy is the father of lies (John 8:44), but God is not the author of confusion (1 Corinthians 14:33). If you're constantly left spinning in self-doubt, not knowing what's true anymore, it's worth asking: *Who benefits from my confusion?*

Gaslighting is not love. It's a tactic of control—and recognizing it is often the first step in reclaiming your clarity, your voice, and your freedom in Christ.

Melissa's Story: The Moving Target

Melissa stood at the kitchen sink, hands still damp from rinsing dishes, when she quietly asked her husband why he hadn't come home the night before.

He scoffed. "What are you even talking about? I was home. You were just asleep—again. As usual."

But she knew he hadn't been. The bed was untouched. The truck hadn't been in the driveway. Still, her heart raced. *Maybe I did fall asleep and miss him coming in. Maybe I'm losing it.*

Later, she found a fast-food receipt in his jeans pocket from a city two hours away, timestamped after midnight. When she showed it to him, he exploded: "Oh, so now you're going through my stuff? That's real Christian of you. You're paranoid. Controlling. This is why I stay away—because nothing I do is ever enough for you."

She apologized, like she always did.

Gaslighting had trained Melissa to doubt her reality. What began as subtle denial and blame-shifting had become a pattern of confusion, emotional withdrawal, and verbal put-downs. He called her crazy. He minimized her hurt. He turned every question into an accusation. Her world began to shrink. She stopped confiding in friends. She stopped trusting her instincts.

On Sundays, he raised his hands in worship. During the week, he raised his voice in contempt.

Melissa started journaling what she knew had happened. She began to name the lies. It was a slow awakening—but one day, she realized that the fog wasn't her fault. It had been placed there.

Emotional abuse leaves no bruises. But its wounds run deep—eroding confidence, mental health, and trust in your own perception of reality.

Financial Abuse

Financial abuse creates dependence by limiting or controlling access to money and resources. It often escalates in tandem with other forms of abuse.

It can look like:

- Refusing to let a partner work.
- Giving an inadequate allowance and demanding receipts.

- Hiding money or rerouting funds without consent.
- Threatening to cut off support during arguments.
- Spending family money recklessly or secretly.

"He wanted to take expensive vacations we couldn't afford and got angry when I said no. More than once, he threatened to empty our joint account without warning. He even moved his Social Security checks to a separate account behind my back—and when bills were due, the money was gone."

Spiritual Abuse

Spiritual abuse twists Scripture, faith, or religious authority to control or silence. It happens when someone uses spiritual language not to build up—but to dominate and degrade.

Examples include:

- Quoting verses to demand submission.
- Saying disagreement equals rebellion against God.
- Claiming divine authority to justify mistreatment.
- Shaming or punishing a partner in God's name.
- Using church teachings to suppress a woman's voice or freedom.

"I was mentoring a younger woman in a difficult marriage. My husband accused me of having an affair with her, which made no sense. Then he told me I was sinful and insisted I read Psalm 51, the psalm of repentance. I couldn't keep helping her. To this day, I struggle to hear that psalm without flinching."

Abuse of Children

Watching your children be harmed—or fearing you can't protect them—is a unique form of trauma. Abuse of children may be verbal, emotional, physical, or neglectful.

Mandated Reporting: If children are being harmed, **you must report it**. Even if you're afraid. Even if you're still in the relationship. This protects your children from further abuse and protects you from being legally considered complicit.

Sexual Abuse in Marriage

Many women have never been told that sexual abuse can exist inside a marriage. The Church has often taught that sex is a duty—something a wife owes her husband—rather than a sacred and mutual expression of love.

But sex without joyful consent is not biblical. It is not loving. It is not holy. It is **abuse**.

Sexual abuse in marriage includes:

- Being pressured, guilted, or manipulated into sex.
- Being touched while asleep when it is unwanted.
- Being grabbed in sexual areas.
- Being shamed for saying no.
- Being forced to perform degrading or painful acts.
- Being told, "Your body belongs to me."
- Being blamed for porn use or affairs.

The so-called "72-hour rule," the idea that men must have sex every three days or suffer physical discomfort, is a lie rooted in pornography, not Scripture. Yet many Christian women are told it's their duty to meet this expectation, no matter how they feel.

"He told me if I refused sex, I had 24 hours to initiate it myself or he would be very upset. I knew what 'very upset' meant."
"He'd come to bed at 3 a.m., aroused, and expect me to be available. I had to get up early with the kids—but that didn't matter to him."
"He required me to say degrading things during sex. It felt humiliating, but I thought that's what a 'godly wife' does to please her husband."

Can There Be Marital Sexual Abuse and Rape?

In Christian marriages, the answer to this question is often whispered—if asked at all. But we must say it clearly:

Yes. Sexual abuse and even rape can happen in a Christian marriage.

It may not look like violence. It may not include threats. It may happen under the guise of prayer, recovery, or Scripture. But if a woman feels used, unsafe, ashamed, or afraid—it is abuse.

Jenna's Silence

Jenna's husband had been clean for nearly a year. Their church praised him. He led men's groups. He shared his testimony. People called him a miracle.

Jenna tried to believe it too.

But at night, he expected sex. If she hesitated, he said, "I'm doing everything right. You're supposed to meet my needs now." If she cried, he called her manipulative. If she resisted, he quoted Scripture: "Don't you believe the Bible?"

She gave in to avoid punishment—the silent treatment, the guilt trips, the subtle threats. Sometimes she numbed herself and went through the motions. It was easier than fighting.

She once hinted at the issue to a ministry leader. The response: "Keep covering him in prayer. Wives are their husband's helper."

Jenna smiled, nodded—and died a little inside.

Then one day she read the word: marital rape. At first, she dismissed it. "It's not that bad. He doesn't hit me." But something inside whispered: This isn't love. And God doesn't ask this of you.

Naming it was the beginning.

When "Submission" Becomes a Weapon

In Christian abuse dynamics, submission is often misused as a weapon. Statements like:

- *"The Bible says to submit."*
- *"Your body belongs to me."*
- *"This is how I stay pure."*

...may sound spiritual—but they are deeply abusive.

God does not endorse coercion. He does not ignore your tears. And He does not call it submission when a woman dissociates, freezes, or cries while her body is being used.

True biblical submission is mutual—rooted in love, not power. Ephesians 5:21 says:

"Submit to one another out of respect for Christ." (CEB)

God never asks a woman to betray her body, her voice, or her safety in the name of faith. That is not submission. That is grief.

The Intersection with Addiction and Recovery

In marriages where a man has battled addiction—especially to porn or sex—abuse can take on unique forms.

He may be "clean" but still expect his wife to meet his fantasy-driven demands. He may use his recovery as a reason to demand sex: *"I need you to help me stay focused."*

He may guilt her with: "Do you want me to relapse?" Or imply that she's withholding love by setting boundaries.

But sobriety is not the same as sanctification. And sex without consent is not intimacy—it is abuse.

"He told me that he's a lot happier just after we have sex, and that things would be easier for me if I made sure to give him what he 'needed.'"

When "Consent" Isn't Really Consent

One of the most overlooked but damaging forms of abuse in Christian marriages is sexual coercion. It doesn't always look like force. It often sounds like persuasion, guilt, or obligation wrapped in spiritual or emotional pressure.

A husband may say things like:

- *"I'm just not myself when I don't get my needs met."*
- *"You're supposed to submit—this is part of your role as a wife."*
- *"Things would go better for you if you weren't always holding out."*

These statements may not come with physical threats, but the impact is just as real. They reduce intimacy to a tool of control, making the wife responsible not only for her husband's mood but also for his entitlement.

If you feel pressured to say "yes" out of fear, guilt, or a desire to keep the peace, that is not true consent.

Sex is not a bargaining chip. It's not owed, forced, or earned. In healthy, godly intimacy, both people are free—free to give, free to decline, free to be fully known and still safe.

Anything less is not biblical love—it's manipulation.

You are not a tool to manage his emotions. You are a whole, image-bearing daughter of God whose body and boundaries matter.

Naming It Is Not Sin

You may be asking yourself:

- Am I overreacting?
- What if I'm dishonoring him by naming this?
- Is it sinful to even think these things?

The answer is no.

Naming abuse is not sin. It is clarity. It is courage. It is the beginning of healing. God sees behind closed doors. He knows your heart. And He does not confuse silence with submission. He does not ask His daughters to be sacrificed on the altar of someone else's desires.

Reflection: If Something Inside You Knows

If your chest feels tight right now... If something deep inside feels disturbed, or seen, or strangely numb... Please hear this: You are not alone. You are not crazy. You are not exaggerating. And you are not betraying your marriage by telling the truth about your pain. God does not sanctify coercion. He does not endorse spiritual manipulation. He does not ignore the tears you cry in silence. And He is not ashamed of your voice.

Now that you've read through the many forms that abuse can take—some loud, others quiet—it may help to reflect gently and honestly on your own experience. The following self-assessment is meant to offer clarity, not condemnation. Let it guide you toward truth and healing.

Personal Awareness Questionnaire: What Have I Lived Through?

Use this self-assessment tool to gently reflect on your experience. There are no right or wrong answers—just opportunities to name what has felt confusing, hurtful, or unsafe. This is not a diagnostic tool but a personal inventory. As you read each statement, circle the response that best reflects your experience.

Response Key: Circle one: **Never / Sometimes / Frequently**

Emotional and Verbal Abuse - I feel like I'm walking on eggshells around my partner. (Never / Sometimes / Frequently)
- My feelings are minimized or dismissed when I try to share them. (Never / Sometimes / Frequently)
- I'm blamed for things that aren't my fault. (Never / Sometimes / Frequently)
- I'm called names or insulted, even in private moments. (Never / Sometimes / Frequently)
- I feel like nothing I do is ever enough to please him. (Never / Sometimes / Frequently)
- He consistently ruins special occasions, including afterwards. (Never/ Sometimes/ Frequently)

Spiritual Abuse - Scripture is used to control me or justify his actions. (Never / Sometimes / Frequently)
- I've been told that questioning his behavior is rebellion against God. (Never / Sometimes / Frequently)
- I've been pressured to forgive without real repentance. (Never / Sometimes / Frequently)
- My church minimized or ignored my concerns about abuse. (Never / Sometimes / Frequently)
- I've been told that submission means staying silent and enduring mistreatment. (Never / Sometimes / Frequently)

Gaslighting and Psychological Manipulation - I'm often confused after conversations and question my own memory or perception. (Never / Sometimes / Frequently)

- He denies saying or doing things I clearly remember. (Never / Sometimes / Frequently)
- I feel like I'm losing touch with what's real or true in the relationship. (Never / Sometimes / Frequently)
- I've been made to feel like I'm the "crazy" one or overly sensitive. (Never / Sometimes / Frequently)
- He changes the subject or flips blame when I try to bring up concerns. (Never / Sometimes / Frequently)

Financial Control - I have little or no access to family money or financial decisions. (Never / Sometimes / Frequently)
- I'm given an "allowance" but must justify all my spending. (Never / Sometimes / Frequently)
- He makes large purchases or hides financial information from me. (Never / Sometimes / Frequently)
- I feel guilty for spending money on basic needs or self-care. (Never / Sometimes / Frequently)
- He uses money to punish me or reward my compliance. (Never / Sometimes / Frequently)

Sexual Coercion or Violation - I feel pressured to have sex even when I'm exhausted, hurting, or unwilling. (Never / Sometimes / Frequently)
- I've been told that meeting his sexual needs will keep the peace. (Never / Sometimes / Frequently)
- I feel used or unseen during sexual encounters. (Never / Sometimes / Frequently)

- Saying no is not respected—or it leads to sulking, anger, or punishment. (Never / Sometimes / Frequently)
- I've given in out of fear, guilt, or obligation, not desire or love. (Never / Sometimes / Frequently)

Physical Abuse or Intimidation - He has grabbed, shoved, or restrained me in anger. (Never / Sometimes / Frequently)
- I've been afraid he might physically hurt me or the children. (Never / Sometimes / Frequently)
- He uses physical closeness, blocking, or towering over me to intimidate. (Never / Sometimes / Frequently)
- I've hidden bruises or injuries or explained them away to others. (Never / Sometimes / Frequently)
- My body no longer feels like a safe place in this relationship. (Never / Sometimes / Frequently)

Control, Isolation, and Intimidation - He makes decisions for me without my input or against my will. (Never / Sometimes / Frequently)
- I feel isolated from friends, family, or outside support. (Never / Sometimes / Frequently)
- He monitors my texts, emails, or whereabouts. (Never / Sometimes / Frequently)
- I'm afraid of how he'll react if I express disagreement or independence. (Never / Sometimes / Frequently)
- He uses silence, threats, or anger to control my choices. (Never / Sometimes / Frequently)

Reflection:

After reviewing your responses, take a moment to sit with what you've seen. Even if only a few of your responses were Sometimes or Frequently, it is likely that you are experiencing significant abuse.

- Were there categories where "sometimes" or "frequently" surprised you?

- Which questions made you feel the most grief—or clarity?

You are not imagining things. If these patterns feel familiar, you are not alone. Help is available, and God's heart is for your safety, truth, and healing. This awareness is not the end—it is the beginning of clarity, strength, and freedom.

Chapter 5 Discussion Questions

1. Which abuse category surprised you most? Why?
2. Have you experienced a *non-physical* abuse tactic that felt worse than a physical blow? Describe its impact.
3. How has Scripture been used to either wound you or bring healing in the context of abuse?
4. Financial control can be hidden. What money practices in your home feel unsafe or secretive?

5. Read Ephesians 5:21–25. How does mutual submission differ from the way "submission" was taught or modeled to you?

6. What is one boundary or safety step you could take this week to honor your body, soul, and spirit?

7. Have you ever felt pressured, guilted, or obligated to say yes to sex in your marriage—even when your heart said no? What messages (spoken or unspoken) made you feel you couldn't say no?

Psalm 34:18: *The Lord is close to the brokenhearted and saves those who are crushed in spirit.*

Chapter 6:

THE POISON OF ENTITLEMENT—"I DESERVE IT" AND THE DESTRUCTION IT BRINGS

Kara's Story: "I Deserve This"

Kara waited for the peace that never came.

For years, she endured the volatility of her husband's drinking—his harsh words, unpredictable moods, and reckless decisions. He blamed his behavior on stress, childhood trauma, and her supposed failures as a wife. "You don't understand what I carry," he'd say. "I work hard. I deserve a break." When things got especially bad, he'd cry and promise to do better. And Kara would hope.

Eventually, he got sober. He started going to recovery meetings. He joined a men's Bible study. He even began sharing his testimony at church, painting himself as a changed man— rescued, redeemed, and on fire for God. "I've turned my life around," he declared from the pulpit. "It's all because of Jesus."

The church rallied around him. Kara heard people say how inspiring he was. A deacon pulled her aside and told her how blessed she must feel. "You're part of his victory story," he said with a smile.

But at home, it was still all about him.

Kara noticed that his demands hadn't gone away—just changed shape. He now expected constant admiration for his sobriety. If she asked him to take responsibility for past harm, he accused her of being unforgiving. "God's forgotten it. Why can't you?" If she said no to sex, he sulked or snapped. "I have needs. You're my wife." If she needed space or rest, he called her lazy and unsupportive. "I'm doing the work—why aren't you?"

He talked endlessly about what he'd earned: her respect, the church's approval, the right to make decisions without question. Sobriety, to him, was a bargaining chip—proof that everyone around him should now comply with his desires.

He treated his recovery like a badge that gave him special privileges. If Kara pushed back, he'd remind her of his progress. "You have no idea what it took to get here," he'd say. "You owe me your trust. You owe me your support."

It took Kara a long time to name what she was living with. This wasn't just selfishness or immaturity. It wasn't about unresolved trauma or a bad day. It was entitlement. A deeply ingrained belief that he was the center of every story, that his efforts earned him devotion, and that other people—especially her—existed to meet his emotional, sexual, and spiritual needs.

He was no longer drinking. But he still believed the world owed him something.

Kara eventually realized that as long as he refused to surrender that belief, nothing would truly change—not in his heart, not in their home.

Entitlement is one of the most destructive, yet least recognized, forces operating beneath both addiction and abuse. It's a mindset—a heart posture—that says. *"I deserve special treatment. I'm owed something. My pain justifies my behavior. The rules don't apply to me."*

This belief system gives a person permission to act without regard for the impact on others It distorts reality, twists relationships, and silences victims. When someone operates from entitlement, they see the people around them not as fellow image-bearers of God with equal value but as tools to meet their own needs—whether physical, emotional, sexual, or spiritual.

In the context of addiction and abuse, entitlement becomes a potent cocktail of self-justification, blame-shifting, and unchecked power. It is a hidden engine behind coercive control, manipulation, rage, and even the misuse of religious language. And perhaps most dangerously, entitlement often survives sobriety. If left unaddressed, it can continue doing deep damage in relationships long after the drugs or alcohol are gone.

Let's look at how this mindset works and why dismantling it is essential for any true healing to take place.

What Is Entitlement?

Entitlement is the belief that I am owed something by others or by life itself. It often includes the idea that normal consequences shouldn't apply to me—*because I've been through so much,* or *because I'm doing better than I used to,* or *because I'm trying.* At its root, entitlement centers on the self and minimizes or erases the experiences of others.

It can sound like:

- "I work hard, so I deserve to blow off steam."
- "You're supposed to support me, no matter what."
- "You should be thankful I'm not doing what I used to."
- "God forgave me. Why are you still holding this against me?"

While it may sometimes come across as self-pity, it's really a demand: *Meet my needs. Validate my experience. Cater to me.*

In healthy relationships, mutual respect and empathy guide our behavior. But in a relationship poisoned by entitlement, one person's needs and feelings dominate the entire emotional landscape.

Entitlement in Addiction

Addiction thrives on the belief that the person in addiction's immediate relief matters more than long-term impact or relational consequences. In this mindset, drugs, alcohol, sex, porn, or gambling become "rewards" or "escapes" the person feels they have earned—because of stress, trauma, or simply because they want it.

An entitled person in addiction may say things like:

- *"You don't understand the pressure I'm under."*
- *"I've been through hell—you'd drink too if you'd lived my life."*
- *"I deserve something for myself."*

This is not to dismiss pain or trauma. Many people struggling with addiction *have* experienced deep wounds. But entitlement distorts that pain into justification for harming others, avoiding responsibility, and refusing accountability. It demands sympathy while offering none.

Worse still, when the person with addiction issues begins a journey of sobriety, this same entitlement can simply shift forms. Instead of, "I *deserve to use*," it becomes, "I *deserve to be admired for my recovery*," or "You *should be over it by now*—I'm sober, aren't I?" The underlying belief—that others owe them something—hasn't changed. It's just wearing new clothes.

Entitlement in Abuse

Entitlement is at the heart of many abusive dynamics. The abusive partner feels he is owed obedience, loyalty, admiration, sex, submission, or silence. He sees his partner not as an equal but as someone who exists to meet his emotional or physical needs. If she resists, he feels justified in punishing her—whether through anger, withdrawal, threats, belittling, or spiritual guilt.

In Christian settings, this becomes especially dangerous. Scripture is twisted to justify entitlement. Passages about headship, forgiveness, or submission are taken out of context and weaponized to control. The abuser may say things like:

- *"The Bible says you have to submit to me."*
- *"You're supposed to forgive—Jesus did."*
- *"You're ruining my testimony by bringing this up again."*
- *"God made me the spiritual leader. You need to follow."*

Entitlement makes repentance impossible. Why? Because true repentance requires humility, grief over harm done, and a willingness to give up power. But entitlement resents being challenged. It demands being seen as "the good guy"—even when harm has been done repeatedly.

When Entitlement Survives Sobriety

Many women in faith communities have experienced this devastating reality: their husband gets sober, starts attending church or recovery meetings, maybe even shares a dramatic testimony—and yet at home, nothing really changes. He's no longer drinking, but he's still controlling. Still selfish. Still demanding. Still cruel.

This is entitlement in action.

Recovery from addiction that doesn't address the entitled mindset is *not* true recovery—it's image management. And sadly, churches often applaud outward sobriety without asking what's happening behind closed doors.

A woman may hear:

- *"Be grateful—he's not the man he used to be."*
- *"Don't you see how much he's changed?"*
- *"He's trying—you need to support him."*

Meanwhile, she's still being mistreated. Her voice is still silenced. Her boundaries are still violated. The *form* of abuse has changed, but the *function*—power and control—remains.

The Impact on the Survivor

Living with an entitled partner takes a deep toll on a woman's soul. She is often made to feel selfish, unspiritual, or unforgiving for needing space, safety, or boundaries. She may constantly second-guess herself: *Am I being too hard on him? Shouldn't I give him more grace?* She may be told by others—and by her own inner critic—that she's bitter or unwilling to move on.

But here is the truth: you are not selfish for saying *no* to being used. You are not unforgiving for wanting to be treated with respect. You are not bitter for remembering the damage someone caused.

Entitlement robs the survivor of oxygen. It requires her to center someone else's needs at the cost of her own. It's not love—it's exploitation dressed up as spiritual obligation.

The Only Cure: Humility, Not Applause

Philippians 2 gives us a radically different picture of how we are called to live:

> *"Do nothing out of selfish ambition or vain conceit. Rather, in humility value others above yourselves, not looking to your own interests but each of you to the interests of the other"* (Philippians 2:3–4).

Jesus, though fully God, did not demand His rights. He humbled Himself and served. That is what real leadership, real love, and real repentance looks like.

Entitlement demands recognition. Humility asks, *"How can I make things right?"*

Entitlement protects self-image. Humility cares more about the other person's healing than about saving face.

Entitlement says, *"You owe me."* Humility says, *"I've caused harm. What do you need from me to heal?"*

Until a person lays down their entitlement—until they stop believing the world owes them something—they cannot truly love others. And they cannot truly change.

For the Survivor: You Are Not Here to Meet His Needs

One of the greatest lies entitlement teaches is that your purpose is to revolve around someone else's wants. That your needs, boundaries, and voice are less important. That speaking up is rebellion. That leaving is betrayal. That resistance is bitterness.

But the truth is: you are not a supporting character in someone else's story. You are not here to be used, absorbed, or erased.

You are a whole person, created in the image of God, with equal dignity, value, and voice. And you have every right—*biblically and relationally*—to expect respect, accountability, and safety in your relationships.

Don't mistake someone's recovery story for actual change. Don't mistake charisma for character. Don't mistake entitlement for leadership. And don't let anyone—no matter how "reformed" they appear—tell you that you're selfish for protecting your own soul.

As we've seen, entitlement is not always loud or obvious. Sometimes it hides behind charm, religious language, or even a recovery story that sounds inspiring on the surface. But when someone believes they are owed special treatment or are above accountability, abuse often follows—no matter how clean, sober, or spiritual they appear. This sets the stage for another confusing and painful experience for many survivors: being told that a mental health diagnosis or personality disorder *explains* or even *excuses* the abusive behavior. When the conversation shifts from responsibility to disorder, it's easy to wonder: Is *this really abuse, or just illness? Is he controlling, or just wounded?* In the next chapter, we'll explore whether a diagnosis changes the moral weight of abuse—and why compassion and accountability must go hand in hand.

Chapter 6 Reflection and Discussion Questions

These questions can be used for personal journaling, support groups, or one-on-one mentoring conversations.

1. **Where have you seen entitlement show up in your partner's words or actions?**
    Were there specific phrases or patterns that revealed an "*I deserve this*" mindset?

2. **Has your partner ever used his recovery, faith, or testimony to avoid accountability?**
    How did that affect your ability to speak up or set boundaries?

3. **What messages have you internalized about your own needs or boundaries?**

   Have you ever felt guilty or selfish for protecting yourself? Where do those beliefs come from?

4. **What does Philippians 2:3–4 show you about the difference between Christlike humility and entitlement?**

   How might this passage reframe the way you view love, leadership, or "submission"?

5. **In what ways has entitlement distorted the relational dynamic in your home, especially after sobriety began?**

   What changed, and what didn't?

6. **If you were to let go of the pressure to please, accommodate, or absorb someone else's entitlement, what might you gain?**

   What would feel frightening about that? What might feel freeing?

7. **How can you begin to reclaim your God-given voice, value, and right to safety—even if others disapprove or misunderstand?**

Chapter 7:

DOES A DIAGNOSIS OF MENTAL HEALTH ISSUES OR PERSONALITY DISORDERS EXCUSE ABUSE?

Introduction

When we talk about the confusion between addiction, mental illness, and personality disorders, sometimes the clearest insight comes through the lived experience of someone who's walked through it. The following story, shared by a woman who endured a year-long marriage filled with addiction, emotional abuse, and psychological manipulation, illustrates how damaging it can be when substance use, narcissistic traits, and spiritual language are blended together.

This account reveals not just how abuse hides behind sobriety—but also how easy it is to get trapped when red flags are minimized, spiritualized, or buried beneath our longing for love and redemption.

Angie's Story: He Was Sober—But I Was Still Being Destroyed

About thirteen years ago, I met him while he was completing a Christian rehab program. I worked at the same site and was still healing from a painful divorce. He was funny, charming, and easy to talk to. He had finished both the rehab and discipleship phases of the program and often talked about how much he missed his four children. I saw someone who seemed changed and ready for a new life.

We started dating quietly after he graduated. He'd been advised to stay single for a while, but I saw that as overly cautious. There were early signs I now recognize as red flags—like hidden cigarettes and driving on a suspended license—but at the time, I told myself he was trying to get his life together.

When he moved to a different part of the state for work, I visited often. He was fun, affectionate, and had a way of making everything feel exciting. We talked about our shared Christian upbringings. I believed he was a loving father who wanted to rebuild his relationship with his kids. When his attorney asked me to supervise his court-ordered visits—since I worked in child protection—I agreed, believing I was helping restore something good.

After nearly a year, we got engaged. But the engagement dragged on with vague excuses and growing instability. I started seeing signs of substance use, emotional distance, and spiritual language used to cover both. At one point, he admitted to using cocaine. He began drinking more, then spending time in the bathroom or basement for long stretches. Strange odors. Empty accounts. Unexplained absences. One night I came home to him attacking his face with a screwdriver because he believed there were worms inside it.

He began obsessing over the idea that I was cheating. He followed me. Questioned my every move. Even brought a retired cop to administer a polygraph test in our home. I passed, but the accusations didn't stop. He demanded I quit my job, shut down my phone, and prove my loyalty over and over. I gave in to far too much, trying to keep the peace.

The emotional abuse was tangled up in spiritual manipulation. He quoted Bible verses about submission and male headship to justify financial control and dominance. When I asked for counseling, he refused. He called it "unnecessary" and said if I truly trusted God and him, I wouldn't need it.

Eventually, I packed my things to leave. But in a moment of weakness, I gave him another chance. We tried again in a new place. But within weeks, the same pattern returned. Our one-year anniversary trip ended in accusations and verbal attacks. I came home and knew—I was done. I left the house, the marriage, and the hope that he would change.

We divorced. Or rather, he asked for an annulment, saying the whole marriage was a lie. I agreed, just to be free. I had to stand in court and testify that I'd entered the marriage not wanting children and had changed my mind—when in truth, I'd always longed to be a mother. Another slap in the face. But I got through it.

Since then, I've been in therapy. I've learned I'm an empath, and that my tendency to care deeply and fix people had become a liability in the wrong hands. I've learned how addiction can

mask deeper personality disorders. I've learned the devastating effects of narcissistic abuse and what it means to reclaim my own voice.

And I've learned that sobriety does not equal safety.

Reflection

Stories like this are far too common—and often silenced. It's easy to dismiss the chaos as just another relapse, or to believe that love, faith, and patience will be enough to turn things around. But what this woman experienced was more than substance use. The patterns of coercion, manipulation, emotional volatility, and paranoia reveal deep-seated dysfunction that sobriety alone cannot fix.

This is why we must talk about narcissistic traits, borderline personality disorder, and the way mental health and addiction can be used as a smokescreen for abuse. Without clarity, survivors blame themselves. They wait for the good version of the person to reappear. They suffer in silence, thinking love demands it.

But love doesn't destroy.
Love doesn't gaslight.
And real recovery doesn't cycle between apology and abuse.

Sobriety may stop the substance—but it doesn't always stop the control. And if there's no accountability, no growth, and no safety, then it's not healing—it's just a pause between storms.

Mental Illness Issues

Many people who go to a secular detox or rehab come out of it with what is termed a "dual diagnosis," usually a combination of bipolar disorder and substance use disorder (SUD). The bipolar diagnosis may or may not be accurate, especially in the context in which it was given. Often, the person sees a psychologist in detox or rehab one time, reports feeling depressed, and is quickly diagnosed, then medicated to "stabilize" them. The thinking is that mood stabilizers or antidepressants will help reduce cravings for the addictive substance tied to their SUD diagnosis.

They may also be placed on maintenance doses of Suboxone or Methadone to deter them from returning to street drugs. But this approach is rarely effective—and certainly not a long-term solution. Many people sell their prescribed drugs to buy what they really want. Others stay on the prescribed drugs but require increasingly higher doses to keep cravings at bay. There is no real freedom in what is called MAT (medically assisted therapy). It can help stabilize someone short-term and get them off the streets long enough to enter a long-term program—but it does not make someone healthy and whole.

Please hear me clearly: there are legitimate diagnoses of bipolar disorder and appropriate use of medication to manage them. Bipolar disorder is a real medical condition that may require a combination of medication and therapeutic support. Unfortunately, however, it has become too easy to categorize people with substance abuse issues in ways that don't help them—and in fact, may cause more harm by masking the deeper issues and making them dependent on medication instead of healing at the root.

The question remains: does mental illness excuse abuse?

The answer is no.

It is never okay to mistreat another person—no matter what.

While people with severe mental illness may at times become violent or unpredictable, that is not an excuse for abusive behavior. If someone is truly unable to control themselves, they need to be in a facility where they and others are safe. But that is not the situation we are addressing in this book.

We are speaking to women whose partners function in public—at work, at church, at family gatherings—but turn abusive behind closed doors. If a person can control themselves in public, **they are capable of choosing how they treat the people closest to them.** Mental illness is not an exemption from accountability.

In an article by Dr. Lisa Aronson Fontes titled "*Abuse Cannot Be Blamed on Alcoholism or Mental Illness,*" she writes:

"Abusers love excuses. They yelled at you because they were drunk. They hit you because they were hit as children. They're abusive because they're depressed. It's not their fault. You should be more understanding. Abusers will not take meaningful responsibility for their behavior. The first step to change is admitting that they are accountable for how they have treated you. Abusers who deny what they have done or who blame it on something or someone else—are not ready to change."[vi]

She goes on to state that while alcohol or drugs may worsen abusive episodes, they are **not the cause** of the abuse.

What About Personality Disorders?

It is helpful to not only look at the **"what"** of abuse and coercive control but also the **"why."** Not every abuser has a diagnosable personality disorder. A person raised in a home where abuse was normalized—especially with a father who mistreated women—may learn to mimic those patterns, especially if he was seeking approval or identity. Generations of men raised in systems that devalue women often display narcissistic tendencies, even without meeting the clinical criteria for a disorder.

Still, it is helpful to understand the types and impact of the most common personality disorders, **not to label or diagnose**, but to give language to a set of behaviors that feel confusing, contradictory, and often traumatizing. It's like trying to walk through a corn maze blindfolded. Having a framework can remove the fog of shame and give women clarity—especially when they are being blamed for the very things that are harming them.

A formal diagnosis of a personality disorder should only be made by a qualified mental health professional. But for those of us navigating relationships, we need tools to name the patterns we see.

There are four types of personality disorders in what psychology categorizes as Cluster B:

- Antisocial Personality Disorder
- Borderline Personality Disorder (BPD)
- Histrionic Personality Disorder
- Narcissistic Personality Disorder (NPD)

Each type has distinct features, but many individuals show traits from more than one. These are not rigid categories—they're behavioral patterns that exist on a spectrum. For instance, someone with narcissistic traits may not completely lack empathy; instead, they may use empathy manipulatively. Adam Young, in *The Place We Find Ourselves* podcast, points out that some bullies have a highly attuned sense of what hurts others—but instead of using that awareness to comfort, they use it to wound more deeply and maintain control.

A diagnosis—or suspected personality disorder—**does not excuse harmful behavior**. The legal system doesn't excuse abuse because of a diagnosis. Neither should we.

There is no excuse for abuse. Period.

For the purposes of this book, we'll focus on narcissistic and borderline traits, as these are the most common in post-addiction abusive relationships. Many women recognize a blend of both in their partner. These traits don't just show up in therapy sessions or psychiatric reports—they show up in everyday conversations, arguments, apologies, and spiritual manipulation.

Understanding Narcissistic and Borderline Traits in the Context of Post-Addiction Abuse

When a partner gets sober, it's natural to hope that everything will get better. And in many cases, it does. But for some women, the outward recovery is only part of the picture. The drinking or drug use may have stopped, but the emotional volatility, manipulation, and spiritual control remain.

This is where things get confusing. A man may be clean and sober—but still use fear, shame, and entitlement to control the woman in his life. And because he's "not using anymore," the abuse gets harder to explain, even to yourself. You might hear things like:

"Why can't you just be proud of him?"
"He's a new creation now, right?"
"Forgive and move on."

But real change is about more than sobriety. It's about safety, empathy, and accountability. Some post-addiction behaviors may line up with what mental health professionals call narcissistic personality disorder (NPD) or borderline personality disorder (BPD). While these are clinical diagnoses that only a qualified professional can make, understanding the patterns can bring clarity when you're feeling spiritually and emotionally trapped.

Narcissistic Traits: When Sobriety Turns into Superiority

A partner with narcissistic traits may be consumed with maintaining an image of success—especially within the church or recovery community. He wants to be seen as the hero of his story—the man who overcame addiction. But at home, he may still act in ways that are deeply harmful, even while appearing spiritual or in control. People with narcissistic traits feel empty inside and are extremely insecure. They look to other people to fill them (narcissistic supply).

I liken a narcissistic person to a black hole in space. Black holes drag in any matter that is in proximity to it, including bright stars, and diminish it to a single pinpoint. It is the same with a narcissistic abuser. There is no amount of filling that will untwist their warped soul. Instead, they will diminish your light until you are destroyed or leave. It is only then that you are not a threat to them anymore.

Narcissistic traits are not always the "grandiose" type that is commonly associated with the disorder. There are multiple types of narcissism, including covert (not so obvious) and vulnerable narcissism. They also can be on a spectrum of mild traits all the way to full-blown NPD.

Signs of narcissistic traits in a post-addiction partner:

- He expects constant praise for his sobriety and may become angry or withdrawn if you don't show admiration.
- He ignores or minimizes the pain he caused during addiction—and may accuse you of being bitter if you bring it up.
- He speaks down to you, using scripture or "spiritual leadership" to justify control.
- He's more invested in how the marriage *looks* than how it *feels*.
- He twists your words to make you feel like you're the problem.
- He rarely apologizes without conditions—and almost never changes behavior in response to your needs.

This kind of dynamic leaves you exhausted and invisible. You may be spiritually shamed for not "submitting" or for not being more supportive. But submission is never meant to be servitude. Real leadership includes humility, repentance, and a willingness to change—not just getting sober.

> "A narcissist will be carrying the Bible in one hand, and a knife in the other. It depends on the audience as to which hand you'll see..."

> @narcissistic_abuse_is_real

Borderline Traits: When Love Is a Rollercoaster

A partner with borderline personality disorder traits often struggles with emotional regulation and deep fears of abandonment. Life is a roller coaster with that person; the ups and downs can alternate extremely rapidly. While his addiction may have numbed those feelings before, sobriety can bring them to the surface—and if he's not in therapy or doing deep emotional healing work, those unresolved issues can explode in your direction.

Signs of borderline traits in a post-addiction partner:

- He swings between adoring you and blaming you, sometimes in the same hour.
- He makes you feel responsible for his moods, identity, or sense of worth.
- He threatens self-harm or abandonment when you set boundaries.
- He creates drama or chaos to test your loyalty or punish you for pulling away.
- He seems deeply insecure one moment, and rageful the next.
- He says he's scared of losing you—but behaves in ways that push you away.

In Christian spaces, this can be confusing. He may cry during worship, talk about being broken before God, and then belittle or isolate you at home. You may feel terrified of what will happen if you stop managing his emotions. It is the ultimate experience of "walking on eggshells." One of the best-known books on Borderline is titled, *I Hate You—Don't Leave Me*, by Jerold Kreisman.[vii] The title says it all so profoundly. Life with someone with BPD is like walking in quicksand. You never know where it is safe to put your foot for the next step. You may be on solid ground and then sink up to your neck in another second. As in narcissism, a person with BPD is a veritable "black hole" of emotional emptiness.

Therapist Jim Cress on the Therapy and Theology podcast (season 8 episode 4) talked about four issues in a person's early years that may contribute to someone developing BPD: abandonment, abuse, addiction, and attachment issues. **We can use this knowledge to understand the person better, but we should be very cautious about trying to diagnose them**.

The other caution is that we may feel obligated to stay in a toxic relationship because the other person has experienced abuse or any of the things on the list, so they can't be held responsible for their behavior. **They are still responsible**. Please hear that clearly! There is a common saying that hurt people hurt people. A better saying would be that hurtful people hurt people. We are not called to be the sacrificial lamb on the altar of their woundedness. There is help available, if someone will make the effort and want change.

Why This Matters

Whether a partner's post-addiction behavior reflects narcissistic or borderline traits—or simply long-standing abusive patterns—the result is the same: you are living in fear, confusion, and chronic emotional exhaustion. You are not imagining this. Abuse does not end when substance use stops. In fact, some women find it becomes even harder to name or leave, especially when others are celebrating his recovery and urging reconciliation.

You deserve more than a sober abuser.

You deserve safety, tenderness, and real transformation—not just a big story.

Sobriety is the beginning of the journey—not the end.

The Dr. Jekyll and Mr. Hyde Confusion

One of the most disorienting experiences in an abusive relationship—especially after a partner gets sober—is the constant cycling between kindness and cruelty. One moment, he's reading his Bible or fixing the kids' lunch. He's charming at church, witnessing to anyone he meets, or praying over dinner. And then suddenly—something shifts. A sharp tone. A hurtful criticism. A silence that speaks loudly. An explosive rage.

It feels like you're living with two different people. That is because you are.

This dynamic is often referred to as the "Dr. Jekyll and Mr. Hyde" pattern. It's named after the classic story in which a man has two selves—one that's polished, respectable, and admired by society, and another that is violent, unpredictable, and hidden. For women in abusive relationships, this shifting can feel like emotional whiplash. You feel adored one minute and despised the next. You find yourself constantly trying to guess which version is going to show up today. You blame yourself. You wonder if you're the crazy one.

This back-and-forth is not accidental—it's part of the cycle of abuse. It is part of what keeps us entangled with someone who is highly manipulative. We see the "good times" as being the real person, the Dr. Jekyll persona. We reason that the bad times (Mr. Hyde) come because of their wounding as a child or their need for further spiritual maturity or whatever excuse we use at that moment. Unfortunately, the truth is that the real person is Mr. Hyde. He knows how to wear a mask at times, but he can't sustain it.

Abusers rarely show their worst sides to everyone. In fact, many are particularly skilled at managing their image. They might be pillars in the church, seen as experts on addiction recovery, or viewed as having a powerful testimony.

But behind closed doors, the mask slips.

Chuck DeGroat talks about "the concept of fauxnerability–when people or systems speak the language of spiritual humility, self-awareness, or emotional health, but lack the real, transformative character change which leads to genuine wholeness and holiness."[viii]

Here's what this can look like:

- He explodes over something small, then later acts like nothing happened.
- He lashes out in a cruel tirade, then brings you flowers and acts affectionate.
- He berates you, then weeps and says he's ashamed and didn't mean it.
- He promises to change, goes to a men's group once or twice, then blames you again for being "unforgiving" when you are not interested in being intimate with him.

This inconsistency creates what's known as intermittent reinforcement, a powerful psychological trap. The good moments give you hope. They make you question yourself. They keep you emotionally invested, believing that if you just love well enough, are perfect enough, or pray hard enough, the "good version" of him will stick around.

But real healing is consistent.

Real repentance produces fruit.

Real love does not leave you afraid, confused, or emotionally shattered.

If someone treats you well only when it benefits them—or only when you're meeting their emotional needs—it is not love. It is control.

The Jekyll/Hyde dynamic is particularly common in people with narcissistic or borderline traits. Their sense of self is unstable, and they often use others to regulate their emotions.

You may feel adored moment and despised the next—not because you've changed, but because they're cycling through their own unresolved wounds and identity issues without taking responsibility.

In Christian communities, this can be spiritualized in harmful ways. You may hear, "*He's struggling with the flesh,*" or "*We all fall short.*" While it's true that everyone needs grace, it is also true that **you are not called to be the sacrifice on someone else's altar of dysfunction**. The sacrifice of Jesus Christ on the cross is sufficient. You don't have to keep carrying the physical, emotional, and spiritual consequences of someone else's unrepentant harm. **A truly good person would never fake abuse, but a toxic person is capable of faking kindness for a time as a manipulation.**

> "*For those who are confused by an abuser's intermittent kindness, just remember: It isn't a miracle. It's a manipulation.*"
>
> Unchained by Hope

Core Traits Within Personality Disorders That Fuel Abusive Dynamics:

Entitlement—demands obedience, justifies control as "deserved" or "God-ordained."

Manipulativeness—uses gaslighting, guilt-tripping, love bombing, or spiritual distortion to destabilize partner.

Lack of Empathy—minimizes the victim's pain, sees them as an object or extension of self.

Emotional volatility—keeps the partner walking on edge—unpredictability, reinforces control.

Grandiosity/Inferiority Flips—abuser may oscillate between superiority and deep shame, projecting insecurity outward through control.

These core traits—entitlement, manipulation, lack of empathy, emotional volatility, and grandiosity—aren't just diagnostic categories. They are lived realities in the homes and hearts of women who have spent years trying to love, serve, and survive men who never truly saw them as equals. These patterns create an emotional climate of confusion, fear, and spiritual weariness—even when no substance is involved.

A man may quote Scripture fluently, serve in church leadership, or even speak publicly about his sobriety journey. But when these traits remain present, healing has not yet happened. This isn't just about a diagnosis—it's about behavior. A man doesn't need a label like "narcissist" or "borderline" for his actions to be damaging and abusive.

Too often, women are told that if their partner is sober, their marriage should be "better." But sobriety without humility, without repentance, without transformed behavior and deep healing, still leaves them walking on eggshells. It still leaves them spiritually isolated, emotionally battered, and privately confused.

This is why it's essential to look beyond outward appearances. The applause of the church, the testimony shared from the pulpit, the well-rehearsed tears during a men's group meeting—**none of these erase the reality of coercive control behind closed doors**. And when the traits listed above continue unchecked, they create a cycle of harm that keeps the victim trapped—not just physically, but emotionally, mentally, and spiritually.

It takes courage to see this truth. It takes even more courage to name it.

Looking Ahead

Understanding that sobriety is not the finish line is essential. As we've seen, emotional volatility, coercive control, and spiritual manipulation can continue long after the last drink or drug. But what happens when the substance is gone, the testimony is public, and the applause from the church grows louder—but he is not truly free. In the next chapter, we'll explore what it means when a man is clean from drugs or alcohol but has "substitute addictions" that deeply impact his wife.

Chapter 7 Discussion Questions

1. **Sobriety vs. Safety**

   After reading Angie's story, what behaviors convinced her it was finally time to leave? Which of those feel familiar—or surprising—to you?

2. **Diagnosis Dilemma**

   Has a mental-health or addiction label ever been used to excuse harm in your life (e.g., "I yelled because I'm bipolar")? How did that shape your response?

3. **Black-Hole Metaphor**

   The chapter compares narcissistic need to a black hole. Which of your own needs or boundaries have been "sucked in" trying to fill someone else's emptiness?

4. **Dr. Jekyll / Mr. Hyde**

   Identify a "mask" your partner shows in public that differs from home. How does that discrepancy affect your credibility with friends, family, or church leaders?

5. **Accountability ≠ Judgment**

   Reflect on Dr. Fontes' line: "Abusers who deny or blame are not ready to change." What would accepting this truth require of you right now—emotionally or practically?

Chapter 8:

CLEAN, BUT NOT FREE

One day you'll tell your story of how you overcame what you went through, and it will be someone else's survival guide."

— Brené Brown

"When someone shows you who they are, believe them."

— Maya Angelou

Patricia's Story:

I used to mark the date every year—his sobriety anniversary. I'd post something on social media, just like he wanted, praising God for another year clean. People would comment things like, "Wow, what a miracle!" or "You must be so proud!" And I was, in a way. I had prayed and begged and cried for years for the drinking to stop.

But no one saw what happened behind our front door after the bottle was gone.

No one saw how he'd slam kitchen cabinets if dinner wasn't timed right, or how I held my breath when I heard his truck pull into the driveway. He didn't need to drink to lose control anymore—his anger was always just under the surface, ready to explode. He called it "just venting," but it always seemed to land squarely on me or the kids.

There were no more hidden vodka bottles, but there were hidden browser tabs. Nights he stayed up in the living room, glued to his phone while I lay in bed alone, wondering what else he was watching that I didn't know about.

He was clean—but I wasn't safe. He had stopped drinking, but he hadn't changed. And the church only ever celebrated his sobriety, never once asking how we were doing, or what sobriety looked like from my side of the bed.

I kept trying to convince myself that I should be grateful. "At least he's sober," I told myself over and over. But somewhere deep down, I knew: this wasn't freedom. Not for me, and maybe not even for him.

When a man stops using drugs or alcohol, it's natural to hope that healing will follow. And sometimes, it does. But for many women, the promised peace never comes. Sobriety brings a new kind of confusion: the substances are gone, but the fear remains. That's because addiction often doesn't end—it morphs. What we call "clean" may simply be a shift in behavior, not a transformation of the heart. In earlier chapters, we looked at how sobriety alone isn't a cure for abuse. Now, we're going to look at what often fills the void: the alternative addictions that take over when the high is gone but the need for control, escape, or emotional relief remains.

Addiction Transfer: The Untreated Soul

Addiction doesn't disappear when the substance goes away. Often, it simply changes form. The outward behavior looks different, but the driving need underneath—the hunger for escape, power, control, affirmation, or numbing—remains untouched. This is the quiet reality many women face: they live with a man who is "clean and sober," but the patterns of addiction have only shifted to something more socially acceptable or harder to detect. This is called **addiction transfer**, and it is heartbreakingly common.

When the deeper wounds of the soul are not addressed, the pain doesn't vanish—it just leaks out in new directions. A man may no longer drink or use drugs, but if he hasn't allowed the Spirit of God to pierce the deeper places of fear, shame, entitlement, and selfishness, those things will resurface—often in the form of compulsive anger, pornography, rigid control, or ministry overdrive. He may even believe he's free, because he no longer fits the cultural picture of an "addict."

But addiction is not just about the substance. It's about what a person runs to when he refuses to surrender to the lordship of Christ. Addiction is a form of idolatry, and in many cases, sobriety just shifts the object of worship—from chemicals to control, from pills to power, from substances to self. The heart still seeks to rule its own kingdom, even if the outside looks different.

For the woman who lives with him, the disorientation is profound. She may feel like she's not allowed to grieve or confront these new behaviors because the addiction everyone could see is technically gone. But if she feels unsafe, unseen, or controlled, she's not imagining it. He may be sober—but he is not well.

Addiction is more than just compulsive behavior—it is a false refuge, a counterfeit shelter that promises relief but delivers deeper bondage. When a man gives up drugs or alcohol but doesn't surrender the inner strongholds that drove him there, he will almost inevitably seek another hiding place.

The human heart is wired for worship, and when it does not worship God in truth, it will latch onto something else—control, sex, rage, recognition, work, or even religious performance. These new "refuges" become idols: not carved statues, but false gods that demand loyalty and offer temporary emotional payoffs. The escape is still the goal—it's just wearing a different mask. As Scripture says, *"Those who cling to worthless idols turn away from God's love for them* (Jonah 2:8). True freedom can't be found in switching addictions. It only comes through surrender, humility, and the painful work of real inner transformation.

One of the most common—and most damaging—alternative addictions that surfaces after substance sobriety is anger. It's often overlooked or even justified, especially if the man is no longer physically violent or is still attending meetings or church services. But for many women, anger becomes the new atmosphere in their home: unpredictable, suffocating, and always just one wrong word or look away from explosion.

Anger Addiction

Anger, when left unchecked, becomes more than just an emotion—it becomes a strategy. It can serve as a drug, releasing adrenaline and dopamine in the brain, offering a momentary high that reinforces the behavior. For some men, especially those who once used substances to discharge stress, shame, or helplessness, rage becomes the substitute outlet. It gives a fleeting sense of power and control, especially when they feel emotionally threatened, exposed, or inadequate. The anger doesn't need to be constant to be abusive. In fact, its unpredictability is what gives it power. A slammed door, a sudden outburst, or a cutting remark followed by silence—these create a climate of fear that keeps the woman in a state of hypervigilance.

This is intermittent reinforcement in action, the same pattern seen in both addiction and abuse cycles. The anger is often followed by a "calm" period—a reset where the man might apologize, act remorseful, or offer just enough warmth to keep hope alive. Over time, this cycle conditions the woman to stay, to adapt, to walk on eggshells in order to avoid triggering another outburst. And because he's no longer drinking or using, outsiders don't recognize the danger. He may even use his sobriety as leverage: "*What more do you want from me?*"

Anger releases endorphins (feel good hormones) in the brain in much the same way as drugs, alcohol, or sex would do.

The Hidden High of Anger

We don't often think of anger as an addiction. Yet for many abusive partners, anger functions much like a drug—providing a rush, a release, and ultimately a craving that becomes harder and harder to satisfy.

When someone explodes in anger, their brain and body are flooded with chemicals. Adrenaline surges through the system, preparing them for a fight. Cortisol, the stress hormone, spikes, sharpening focus and heightening the senses. But most interestingly, the brain also releases endorphins, the body's natural painkillers, which create a sense of relief or even euphoria. Add to this the release of dopamine, the brain's reward chemical, and you have a potent neurochemical cocktail that reinforces the angry outburst.

Over time, this pattern can become addictive. The person learns, consciously or unconsciously, that blowing up gives them a chemical "high"—a feeling of release, power, or satisfaction. Even when they feel remorseful afterward, the brain begins to crave the next outburst. Like other behavioral addictions, anger addiction requires stronger and stronger emotional reactions to produce the same effect. The angry person may start provoking conflicts or exaggerating grievances just to feed the craving for that internal rush.

This is one reason why apologetic words after an angry episode don't necessarily signal true change. Without addressing the addictive pull of anger itself—and the underlying wounds or patterns driving it—the person will likely continue the cycle, chasing the next high of control, rage, or emotional release.

I used to believe his apologies because they sounded so sincere. After every outburst, he would hold me and tell me how sorry he was, how much he hated himself for hurting me. But what I didn't realize back then was that he needed the anger and he needed to apologize. It was like watching a balloon inflate and deflate—he had to blow up to let the pressure out, and then he needed the comfort afterward. For years, I thought if I could just help him calm down, if I could be more patient, it would stop. But it never did. It was a cycle—and he was addicted to the release, not interested in real change.

For the victim, it's crucial to understand that these angry explosions are not just "bad moods" or momentary lapses. They are part of a deep, self-reinforcing pattern that can only be broken through serious accountability, surrender to God, and often professional intervention. Anger addiction cannot be managed by sheer willpower; it must be replaced with true heart-level change and the renewal of the mind through the Holy Spirit.

This pattern is often described as "dry drunk" syndrome—a term used to describe individuals who have stopped using substances but still exhibit the same emotional immaturity, control issues, and selfish behaviors that defined their addiction. While the substance is gone, the entitlement remains. He may believe that his sobriety alone should earn him praise, peace, and unquestioned loyalty from those around him. Any challenge to his behavior feels like betrayal. He may see himself as the one who did the hard work, while the woman is expected to simply move on and stop complaining.

Entitlement becomes the driving force behind much of the anger. He believes he deserves comfort, admiration, and control because he's no longer using. And when he doesn't get those things—when life still feels hard, or his wife sets a boundary, or someone questions his behavior—the resentment boils over. Anger becomes a tool to punish, silence, or reassert dominance.

Anger addiction is especially insidious in Christian circles, where it is often excused as "just being passionate" or blamed on stress, past trauma, or a short temper. But Scripture speaks clearly: "*Human anger does not produce the righteousness that God desires*" (James 1:20). Habitual, controlling anger is not a personality quirk. It is a sign of bondage, not freedom. It reveals a man who has not surrendered his emotions to Christ, and who is still relying on fear and force rather than humility and repentance. It reveals an enormous sense of entitlement.

For the woman living in this dynamic, the emotional toll is enormous. She may begin to believe that she is the problem—that if she were quieter, holier, less sensitive, or more submissive, the anger would stop. But the anger is not about her. It is about him—and the broken places he has not allowed God to touch.

Pornography

For many men who once numbed their pain or fed their ego through substances, the pull toward pornography can become the next stop on the addiction carousel. Porn offers immediate escape, stimulation, control, and a sense of power—all without the visible consequences of drugs or alcohol. In Christian homes, it is often hidden, justified, or minimized, especially if the man is "doing better" in other areas. But for the woman, it is another kind of betrayal—one that wounds just as deeply.

Pornography addiction is not a harmless private habit. It reshapes the brain, distorts intimacy, and reduces a woman's God-given identity to something consumable. It teaches entitlement and trains men to expect sexual availability without relationship, mutuality, or emotional responsibility. Dr. Andrew Bauman refers to it as a pornified style of relating—it is pervasive throughout the whole relationship. In some homes, porn is paired with coercion—where the wife is pressured to perform, submit, or accommodate fantasies she's uncomfortable with, all under the guise of being "a good wife." This isn't intimacy. It's exploitation.

For the woman, the impact of ongoing pornography use is betrayal trauma. She may feel degraded, confused, ashamed, or even begin to question her own value. In Christian environments, she may be counseled to "meet his needs" more faithfully, while the deeper issue—his unrepentant behavior and refusal to honor her dignity—is left untouched. No amount of sexual frequency with his wife will change his addiction. In fact, there is often a decrease or absence of desire in a man for his wife when he is using pornography to satisfy himself sexually. A real-life human woman, in this case, is no match for the airbrushed, sexually tantalizing, endless variety of fantasy women available for free.

Sexual sobriety is not just the absence of pornography. It is the presence of *honor*. It is a man who treats his wife as a co-heir of grace, not as an object for consumption or a tool for regulation. Anything less is not recovery—it's a spiritual counterfeit.

Affairs

Several of the brave women who shared their stories with me had entered marriage full of hope—believing they were beginning a godly life with a man who had been freed from addiction. But for some, that hope was shattered when they discovered their husbands were involved with other women.

Though the abuse prior to these discoveries may not have been overtly physical, verbal, or spiritual, the trauma of betrayal hit on all those levels. These were men who were speaking in churches, going on mission trips, and being praised as "trophies of grace"—all while living a double life, deceiving their wives, and eventually abandoning them.

"I thought I was crazy. He kept telling me I was insecure and imagining things. But deep down, I knew something was off. When the truth came out, I felt like I had been living in a house of mirrors."

"He was everyone's success story. They paraded him around the church, gave him microphones and platforms. Meanwhile, I was quietly dying inside, holding the pieces of a marriage that wasn't real."

"The betrayal was more than just the affair. It was the spiritual gaslighting—the way he used God's name to keep me silent and compliant. I didn't just lose a husband. I lost my sense of reality, my community, and my safety."

Betrayal trauma is real—and it often strikes in the context of what looks like a "redeemed" marriage. In these stories, infidelity was not just a moment of moral failure. It was a symptom of deeper patterns of deception, entitlement, and emotional unavailability that never truly got addressed after sobriety. Recovery from addiction had occurred—but transformation of character had not.

Workaholism and Ministry Addiction

Not all addictions look destructive on the surface. In fact, some of the most insidious ones are celebrated—especially in Christian communities. When a man throws himself into long hours at work, nonstop ministry activity, or constant productivity after getting sober, it can look like progress. From the outside, it may seem like he's finally taking responsibility or serving the Lord. But when work or ministry becomes a way to escape real growth, avoid emotional connection, or feed a need for control and admiration, it's not recovery—it's workaholism. It's ministry addiction. And it's deeply damaging.

These forms of addiction are particularly deceptive because they receive applause, not concern. A man who is constantly busy may be praised for his discipline, his leadership, or his "heart for the Lord." But back at home, his wife is left emotionally abandoned. He's unavailable, dismissive, or exhausted—too preoccupied with his next task or next sermon to engage with the actual people in his life. His value comes from how much he's doing, not the person he's becoming. And any attempt to confront this imbalance may be met with spiritual deflection: "*I'm doing God's work.*"

Sometimes ministry addiction is used to manage image. After substance sobriety, he may feel pressure to maintain a testimony, prove he's changed, or compensate for past failure. Rather than letting God reshape him slowly and deeply, he jumps into visible service, building platforms instead of character. Ministry becomes performance. And anyone who threatens that image—especially his wife—is seen as a distraction or enemy.

Meanwhile, the woman feels lonely, unseen, and spiritually gaslit. She may begin to believe that *she* is the one with a bad attitude for wanting time, presence, or partnership. In churches that idolize busyness and "calling," she may be told to support him better, not realizing she is being sacrificed on the altar of his unresolved issues.

But God does not call men to neglect their families or emotional maturity in the name of service. As Paul writes in 1 Corinthians 13:2, *"...if I have a faith that can move mountains, but do not have love, I am nothing."* God is not impressed by a man's ministry resume if love, humility, and repentance are absent at home.

Technology and Gaming Addiction

After substance sobriety, some men turn not to overt control or anger—but to passivity. Rather than exploding, they disappear. Technology and gaming addiction offer a socially acceptable, low-conflict escape hatch from emotional engagement and personal growth. For men who once relied on substances to numb pain or avoid responsibility, endless scrolling, gaming, streaming, or online rabbit holes become the new way to disconnect.

At first glance, this form of addiction may seem harmless. He's not yelling. He's not drinking. He's not cheating. But he's also not *present.* He comes home and immediately plugs into a screen, tuning out the world around him. Conversations are one-sided. Spiritual interest disappears. Parenting becomes minimal. The home becomes a place where he exists—but does not *engage.*

For the woman living with this pattern, the loneliness is consuming. She may sleep next to him every night and still feel completely alone. When she tries to express her hurt, she may be told she's nagging, overreacting, or expecting too much. Over time, the message is clear: the screen matters more than she does.

In some homes, this addiction also manifests as infantilization—a refusal to take on adult responsibilities, especially emotional ones. He may act like a teenage boy rather than a grown man, defaulting to entertainment, comfort, and personal gratification instead of rising into the call to love, protect, and serve. She may find herself "mothering" him instead of partnering with him, carrying the emotional and spiritual burden for the entire household.

Technology is not evil in itself—but when it replaces intimacy, accountability, and growth, it becomes a barrier to love. Addiction to screens is still addiction. It is avoidance dressed in convenience. And just like other false refuges, it must be named before it can be surrendered.

Scripture reminds us that passivity has consequences. Proverbs 18:1 says, "*Whoever isolates himself seeks his own desire; he breaks out against all sound judgment*"(ESV). A man who disappears repeatedly into his devices is not just "unwinding"— he is avoiding. And avoidance never leads to transformation.

Prescription Drug Misuse: Hidden Behind the Label

Not all substance use ends when a man claims sobriety. For some, prescription drug misuse becomes a new, socially acceptable avenue for escape. Pain pills, anti-anxiety medications, stimulants, or sleep aids are framed as "necessary" for physical or mental health—but the patterns that emerge tell a different story. While legitimate medical issues may exist, the exaggeration or manipulation of symptoms to obtain medications can signal a deeper issue: addiction in disguise.

This form of addiction is particularly difficult for women to speak out about. After all, who questions a doctor's prescription? If her husband says he's in pain, she may feel guilty for doubting him. But when the medications become central—when they're guarded, demanded, or taken more than prescribed—something is wrong. He may "doctor shop," self-medicate, or emotionally spiral if the medication is delayed or questioned. These are not the actions of someone simply managing a health issue. These are the red flags of dependence.

In some cases, the man may genuinely believe he needs the medication and resist any conversation about overuse. He may even frame his wife as unsupportive or unspiritual for expressing concern. The prescription becomes his shield— proof that he's not "using" in the way he used to. But the emotional and relational impact remains the same: withdrawal, volatility, detachment, blame-shifting, and a refusal to take full responsibility.

This kind of hidden addiction also feeds entitlement. He may expect special treatment, rest, or avoidance of responsibilities because of his "condition." Any challenge or boundary may be met with defensiveness or rage. The medications become a way to avoid not only physical discomfort but also emotional work, spiritual accountability, and relational maturity.

The woman in this situation often feels trapped. She's labeled critical or cold if she voices concern, yet she lives with the emotional chaos and instability that come with addiction. It's a lonely place—especially in Christian communities where medical issues are often treated with blanket sympathy, while the woman's reality is minimized.

But addiction is not defined by the label on the bottle—it's defined by the fruit it bears. If the behavior isolates, controls, or destabilizes the home, it is not healing—it is harm. Proverbs 4:23 says, "*Guard your heart, for everything you do flows from it.*" When medication is used to guard pain rather than open the heart to God's healing, it becomes a barrier to true freedom.

Food, Exercise, or Body Image Obsession

In some cases, the post-addiction shift doesn't look dramatic or destructive at all—it looks disciplined. Clean eating, strict workout regimens, supplement stacks, or intense focus on physical appearance can seem like signs of health and maturity. But when these things become compulsive, all-consuming, or self-glorifying, they reveal another false refuge. Addiction hasn't left—it has just moved into the mirror.

For men who once abused substances to feel powerful, desirable, or in control, fitness and food can become new idols. The attention shifts from internal transformation to external perfection. He may now obsess over macros, muscle mass, fasting, or routines—and expect those around him to conform or admire him for it. His body becomes a project, and often, a source of pride. In some cases, he may shame his wife for her appearance or demand that she "keep up" with his standards. The focus isn't on mutual well-being—it's on image management.

For others, it's not the pursuit of the perfect physique but obsessive eating habits that become the next form of addiction. This can show up as extreme food restrictions, compulsive eating cycles, or an over-dependence on specific types of food for comfort, especially sugar. Sugar mimics some of the dopamine responses that drugs and alcohol once provided. For men coming off substances, sweets or highly processed carbs often become the new high. It might look innocent—stockpiles of candy, late-night binges, constant snacking—but it's often a numbing mechanism, a substitute stimulant that still feeds the reward pathways in the brain. The mood swings, irritability, and withdrawal-like symptoms remain, even if the substance is technically legal.

In Christian circles, this behavior is often laughed off or overlooked. "Better sugar than alcohol," some will say. But addiction is not about the item—it's about the dependence. If a man needs a cupcake or a protein shake to regulate his emotions, avoid hard conversations, or reward himself for basic responsibilities, he's not living in freedom—he's still looking for a fix.

This obsession—whether with food restriction, overcon-sumption, or physique—often ties into King Baby Syndrome: emotional immaturity, entitlement, and a demand to be admired or catered to. His identity becomes wrapped in appearance or gratification. Meanwhile, the woman he lives with often feels either invisible or used—expected to support his lifestyle while her own needs are ignored.

While taking care of one's body can be good stewardship, body worship and food fixation distort that calling. They prioritize vanity over virtue, comfort over growth, and self-focus over service. And for the woman who lives with it, the message is clear: your worth is measured in comparison. You're not a partner—you're a prop. If you question it, you're "unsupportive." If you ask for more emotional connection, you're "too much."

Underneath it all is the same pattern found in every other addiction transfer: avoidance. As long as he's focused on calories, sugar, or routines, he doesn't have to face his soul. He doesn't have to examine how he treats people. He doesn't have to look at what still needs surrendering. He's "clean"—but he's still not free.

Paul warns against this kind of empty discipline in Colossians 2:23: "*Such regulations indeed have an appearance of wisdom, with their self-imposed worship, their false humility and their harsh treatment of the body, but they lack any value in restraining sensual indulgence.*" In other words, appearance without heart change is nothing more than a shiny form of bondage.

The "Recovery Expert": Power, Platform, and the Illusion of Change

After sobriety, some men quickly pivot into public recovery roles—sharing their testimony, offering counsel to others, or even leading addiction groups. At first glance, this seems like redemption in action: a man who was once lost is now helping others find freedom. And in many cases, it *is* beautiful. True healing leads to humility and service. But for others, this move into the spotlight is not about healing—it's about image management and control. It's about becoming the expert, the authority, the one with all the answers—while still neglecting or mistreating the people closest to him.

These men may build entire personas around their transformation story. Their testimony becomes rehearsed and polished, delivered with emotion and drama. They know what lines make people cry, when to mention God, and how to frame their past in a way that garners admiration. But inside the home, a different story is playing out: spiritual arrogance, emotional withdrawal, or continued abuse. The man who speaks with conviction in a group setting may belittle his wife at the dinner table. The one who talks about grace and growth may fly into rage behind closed doors.

This dynamic creates deep cognitive dissonance for the woman. She sees others praising him for his wisdom, quoting his insights, even seeking him out for guidance—while she feels invisible, gaslit, or silenced. If she speaks up, she risks being labeled bitter, unsupportive, or even spiritually rebellious. *"He's helping so many people—can't you just be happy for him?"* becomes the subtle or direct rebuke.

What often underlies this public "expert" posture is a fragile ego. He craves affirmation and control, and recovery leadership gives him both. It allows him to stay in the center of the story—admired, followed, in charge. But true transformation isn't proven by how many people listen to a man talk about addiction—it's revealed in how he lives, how he loves, and how he responds when no one is watching.

This misuse of testimony and leadership is particularly dangerous in Christian circles, where platforms and "powerful stories" are often idolized. But God is not impressed by eloquence. He looks at the heart. Isaiah 29:13 warns, *"These people come near to me with their mouth and honor me with their lips, but their hearts are far from me."* A powerful testimony without humility, repentance, and consistent love is not transformation—it's theater.

For the woman living in this confusion, know this: you are not crazy for feeling the gap between his public words and private actions. You are not dishonoring him by telling the truth. And you are not required to be the silent cheerleader while he builds a platform on unfinished healing.

Freedom vs. Functioning

Sobriety is not the same thing as freedom. Many men function quite well after giving up substances. They hold jobs. They attend church. They may even lead ministries or speak publicly about their journey. But functioning is not the goal of redemption. God does not call us to merely behave better—He calls us to be made new.

A man may appear to be doing all the right things externally while still living in bondage internally. He may function without alcohol, but still rely on rage, control, pornography, or workaholism to regulate his emotions and protect his ego. He may no longer be intoxicated, but he's still driven by entitlement. He may be clean, but not kind. Present, but not connected. Charismatic in public, but cold and cruel at home.

Women in these relationships often feel intense guilt or confusion. *"He's sober. Why am I still so anxious?"* *"Everyone says he's changed. Why do I still feel so small?"* These questions are not signs of ungratefulness or bitterness. They are signs that something is still deeply wrong. Healing cannot be measured only by the absence of a substance. It must be measured by the presence of love.

Galatians 5:1 declares, *"It is for freedom that Christ has set us free."* Not for image. Not for function. Not for leadership or applause. Freedom means wholeness of heart, consistency of character, and the willingness to love sacrificially—not just speak about it. If those things are missing, the man may be functioning—but he is not free.

For the woman, this truth is critical. You are not unspiritual for longing for safety. You are not asking too much when you hope for more than just sobriety. You were created for relationship that reflects Christ—not one that revolves around someone else's unhealed ego.

A Word to the Woman Living with This

Dear sister, if you are reading this and feeling a knot of recognition in your stomach, I want you to know—you are not imagining it. You are not bitter. You are not crazy. You are not failing God because you are still hurting after his sobriety.

You may have been told that his recovery is your miracle—that now everything should be fine. Maybe you've even told yourself that. You've tried to quiet your own fear, ignore the sharp words, excuse the silence, overlook the mood swings, and "be grateful" because the substance is gone. But you know the truth. You feel it in your body, in your soul, in the way you tense when he walks into the room. Something is still not right.

You are not wrong for wanting more than just the absence of addiction. God designed marriage to be a place of mutual love, safety, and honor—not a recovery center for someone who refuses to grow. Your desire for connection, kindness, emotional safety, and real intimacy is not selfish. It's godly. It reflects the very heart of Christ, who calls His people into relationship marked by gentleness, truth, and faithfulness—not manipulation, performance, or fear.

If your husband has substituted one addiction for another and is now hiding behind his testimony, his service, or his leadership while continuing to harm you—you are allowed to name that. You are allowed to grieve that. You are even allowed to step back from it in order to protect your heart, your mind, and your children. God does not ask you to submit to bondage. He asks you to walk in the light.

Jesus sees the whole story—not just the part that's on stage. He sees behind the recovery glow, the group leadership, the social media posts, and the spiritual-sounding phrases. He sees the man who still refuses humility, and the woman who feels erased in the process. And He calls you by name. El Roi—the God who sees—has not missed a single moment of your silent tears.

You don't have to wait for someone else to validate your pain in order to take it seriously. God already does. And you don't have to wait for someone else to call it abuse in order to protect your soul. He already is. His heart is not only for the one in addiction. His heart is also for the ones the addicted person has wounded—and that includes you.

Chapter 8 Discussion Questions

1. **"He's Clean Now—So Why Am I Still Hurting?"**
   Are there ways you've felt dismissed or silenced because your partner is sober, even though the pain continues? What do people around you assume about your situation?

2. **The "Big Testimony" Trap**
   Has your partner's recovery story been used to minimize or overshadow your suffering? What pressure have you felt to protect his image—even at the cost of your truth?

3. **Image vs. Reality**

   How does your partner behave in public compared to at home? What toll does it take on you to maintain or explain away that difference?

4. **Spiritual Exhaustion**

   In what ways has your faith been impacted by the ongoing abuse? Have you ever questioned God's justice or presence because of how others spiritualized your suffering?

5. **Words That Wound**

   Which phrases—spiritual or otherwise—have been used to justify harmful behavior or shut down your concerns? How have those words affected your ability to speak up?

6. **Redefining Freedom**

   What would *freedom* actually look like for you? Not just for him to stop using, but for you to feel safe, heard, and whole?

Chapter 9:

INTERMITTENT REINFORCEMENT AND TRAUMA BONDING: THE INVISIBLE CHAINS OF ABUSE AFTER SOBRIETY

Sarah's "Changed" Husband

Sarah had prayed for years that her husband would get sober. The drinking brought out a version of him she didn't recognize—angry, reckless, demeaning. He would disappear for hours, sometimes days, and come back with apologies and promises. Each time, she would forgive him, clinging to the hope that the man she married was still in there somewhere.

When he finally entered a Christian recovery program and came out clean, the whole church celebrated. He gave his testimony on a Sunday morning, voice trembling as he thanked God and praised his wife for never giving up on him. People hugged her in the lobby, telling her how lucky she was. How strong. How faithful.

But at home, things didn't feel like a miracle.

The drinking stopped, but the mood swings didn't. He grew cold and condescending when she questioned anything. He used Scripture like a weapon, quoting "wives submit to your husbands" whenever she pushed back. He didn't yell much anymore, but he mastered the art of the cutting silence—withholding affection and attention for days, then suddenly flipping the switch, calling her "babe," holding her hand at dinner, praying over the kids.

She was dizzy with confusion. "Why do I still feel so afraid?" she asked her Bible study leader once. "He's sober. He says he loves God. But I feel like I'm losing pieces of myself."

What she didn't know then was that she was experiencing intermittent reinforcement and trauma bonding. The erratic mixture of withdrawal, blame, and occasional tenderness had rewired her emotional reflexes. She had become addicted—not to love, but to the hope of love. Her brain lit up when he smiled again, like she had finally done something right. And she held onto that fleeting smile with both hands, even when the cost was her voice.

The Hook That Keeps You Hoping: Intermittent Reinforcement

One of the most powerful psychological traps in an abusive relationship is something called **intermittent reinforcement**. It's a term from behavioral psychology, but in real life, it plays out like this: you never know when the next "good moment" will come, so you cling to the hope that it *will*. The unpredictable pattern of reward and punishment wires your brain to chase the highs, even while you're drowning in lows.

It's the same principle behind gambling addiction—where the occasional win keeps the gambler playing far longer than a steady stream of losses ever would. In relationships, this often looks like long stretches of criticism, coldness, or control, followed by sudden affection, apology, or even a glimpse of the man you fell in love with. That's when you think: *maybe he really is changing. Maybe God is working on him. Maybe if I can just hold out a little longer...*

This cycle is not accidental. Whether consciously or unconsciously, abusers use intermittent reinforcement to keep their partners off balance and emotionally dependent. You begin to live for the crumbs—the brief return of warmth, the unexpected "I love you," the tearful prayer of repentance. These moments become more intoxicating because they follow deep emotional starvation.

One woman shared:

I remember one night he screamed at me so viciously that I locked myself in the bathroom, shaking. But two days later, he came home with flowers and a note that said, 'You're my safe place. I'm so sorry I scared you.' He even cried. And I felt relieved. Grateful, even. Like maybe this time the change would stick.

That moment erased the fear—for a little while. I told myself, this is why you stay. This is what love is supposed to fight through. *And at church that week, when the pastor preached on forgiveness, I felt like God was confirming it.*

But then the cycle started again. The yelling. The blame. The silence. The next apology.

I started to feel like a gambler who couldn't leave the table. Every once in a while, he would be that kind, funny, passionate man I married. And I would think, there he is. And I'd cling to it like a lifeline—like maybe if I just prayed harder, waited longer, forgave more, I'd get that version of him full-time.

But I never did. I lived for the highs. And they cost me years of my life.

Dr. Jekyll, Mr. Hyde... and Jesus?

This pattern echoes what we looked at in Chapter 8—the Dr. Jekyll and Mr. Hyde confusion. Just when you think you're ready to leave Mr. Hyde, Dr. Jekyll shows up with a bouquet, a Bible, and maybe even tears. He quotes scripture. He says he knows he's failed. He reminds you of how far he's come since addiction. And maybe he has. But the cruelty still leaks out, hidden behind just enough tenderness to keep you unsure.

This is where spiritual language can deepen the trap. You may be told to "focus on the good," to "remember how far he's come," or to "stand in the gap for him in prayer." If he's been clean from addiction for a while, the pressure to stay gets even heavier. You're no longer just dealing with an abusive partner—you're dealing with someone who has a *testimony*.

A story of redemption. One that people around you may be invested in preserving.

But here's the truth: someone being *sometimes* kind does not cancel out the harm they cause the rest of the time. Kindness isn't a reward—it's a baseline. Real change doesn't swing back and forth like a pendulum. You should not have to gamble your peace or safety for the sake of fleeting moments of love.

What you're really experiencing is a system of emotional addiction. Not because you're weak—but because your brain is doing exactly what it's designed to do: seek connection, avoid pain, and hope for love.

One of the cruelest ironies in emotionally abusive relationships—especially those that continue after a partner gets clean—is how powerful the *good days* can be.

He's sober now. Maybe even going to meetings, quoting Scripture, telling his testimony. And in between the anger, the cold silences, or the manipulative blame-shifting... he brings home flowers. He puts his hand on your shoulder during worship. He tells the kids a bedtime story, then turns to you with soft eyes that say, "*See? I'm changing.*"

This is intermittent reinforcement—the kind of reward that shows up just often enough to keep you hanging on. This pattern is what makes slot machines so addictive: the payout is unpredictable, so we keep pulling the lever, hoping this time will be the one that gives us what we long for.

In relationships, it looks like this:

- One moment: cruelty, blame, silence, or even rage.

- The next: charm, affection, apologies, or spiritual language that sounds sincere.

The unpredictability wires your brain to crave the next "good" moment. And because it's inconsistent, your mind attaches more value to it. You start to feel like you've earned his affection when it comes. And that maybe, just maybe, if you're more patient, more understanding, or godlier... it'll happen more often. This leads to trauma bonding.

Trauma bonding is not a reflection of love—it's a survival response to inconsistent harm. It's what happens when someone hurts you, then comforts you just enough to make you question your memory and suppress your instincts.

Trauma Bonding

Lisa and the Man with the Testimony

Lisa met him at church. He stood up on a Sunday morning and told his story—years of addiction, rock bottom, then Jesus. The room went silent as he spoke, then erupted in applause when he talked about being "delivered." He quoted Scripture fluently, talked about accountability, and said he wanted to be a godly husband and father someday.

Lisa had grown up in church but had her own painful past, and something about his brokenness—and his redemption—made her feel like they spoke the same language. He pursued her gently, prayed with her, and told her she made him want to be a better man. They married quickly.

In the beginning, he seemed like everything she had hoped for: spiritual, humble, passionate about the Lord. But after the wedding, the dynamic started to shift. He became critical, especially about her faith. He'd interrupt her prayers, mock her opinions, and accuse her of being "too emotional" or "rebellious" when she disagreed with him. When she cried, he'd roll his eyes and say things like, "This is why God put me in charge—you can't handle truth."

But then—just as suddenly—he'd swing back toward tenderness. He'd buy her a book on godly marriage. He'd hold her hand in church, lift his hands in worship, and post Bible verses on Facebook about loving your wife as Christ loved the church. To outsiders, he looked like a spiritual leader. To Lisa, he was a riddle she couldn't solve.

When she tried to confide in a mentor, she was told that "all marriages are hard" and "he's just growing—be patient." Lisa started to wonder if she was the problem. Maybe she was too sensitive. Maybe she didn't understand spiritual authority. Maybe she wasn't giving him enough grace.

What she couldn't name yet was intermittent reinforcement— the cycle of criticism followed by care, anger followed by calm, emotional withholding followed by just enough tenderness to keep her hoping. And beneath it all, a deepening trauma bond was forming. She didn't feel safe, but she couldn't walk away. She wasn't being hit, but she felt smaller every day. And in a community that saw him as a spiritual success story, she

didn't know how to explain the quiet kind of harm that had settled into her home.

Trauma bonding is the *natural* (though tragic) result of intermittent reinforcement. This pattern mirrors what research has found to be one of the most powerful ways to keep someone hooked: never knowing when the next "good" moment will come. The very unpredictability of the abuser's behavior *increases* the survivor's emotional investment and anxiety.

This is the trap of trauma bonding—a strong emotional attachment that forms between a victim and their abuser during cycles of abuse, punctuated by intermittent kindness. It doesn't form despite the abuse but *because* of it. That cycle of harm followed by warmth conditions your nervous system to associate emotional survival with staying connected to the very person hurting you.

You don't just want the relationship to work—you *need* those "good" moments to survive the bad ones. You start believing that if you could just behave the right way, or say the right thing, maybe you could unlock the version of him that appears after the blow-ups: the tender one, the worshiping one, the apologetic one.

But those crumbs of connection are not healing. They're bait.

Trauma bonding is not a reflection of love—it's a survival response to inconsistent harm. It's what happens when someone hurts you, then comforts you just enough to make you question your memory and suppress your instincts.

And when the addiction has faded into the background, but control and manipulation remain, this bond can be even harder to break—because now, everyone around you thinks the danger has passed. "He's sober now," they say. "Give it time." What they can't see is the prison built on hope — hope handed to you in just the right dosage to keep you quiet, compliant, and confused.

Have you experienced your partner lavishing you with praise and affection, apologies, gifts, and romantic gestures, only to turn quickly to lashing out, emotional/verbal battering, or physical assault? This is known as the idealization/devaluation/discard cycle.

This cycle can be seen in all types of abusive relationships but is especially obvious in relationships where one partner has narcissistic tendencies or has BPD. The pattern goes as follows:

Tension building—you can sense that things aren't smooth or peaceful but nothing overt has happened yet. A general air of criticism and unhappiness can be felt, especially when you have been through the cycle before. This phase could be likened to a volcano that is showing signs of an upcoming eruption in subtle ways.

Incident—this is often seen as the explosion phase, where the anger volcano goes off and spews its red-hot lava all over those in proximity—usually you and/or the kids.

Reconciliation—this could be considered the flowers and chocolates phase, where words of repentance, gifts, spiritual "remorse," and promises to change takes place. This could be seen as the clean-up after the volcano erupts. Or he may act as if nothing ever happened.

Calm—Dr. Jekyll reappears, and you wonder if you imagined it all. The wonderful person you thought you were marrying emerges, and you imagine that it will never happen again if you can just be perfect enough, do everything he wants, keep the kids from bugging him, and...fill in the blanks. But it never lasts.

Trauma Bonding vs. Codependency: Why It Matters

Far too many women are told they're codependent when, in reality, they're caught in something much deeper and more insidious: trauma bonding. The difference isn't just semantics—it affects how we respond, how we heal, and how we see ourselves in light of God's truth.

Codependency is often described as an unhealthy reliance on another person—seeking self-worth through fixing or enabling them, sacrificing boundaries, or feeling responsible for their emotions or actions. It's rooted in a deep desire to be needed, often stemming from childhood roles and patterns. In a codependent relationship, both parties may unconsciously collude in maintaining dysfunction: one person enables, and the other exploits.

But trauma bonding is different. It occurs in the context of abuse. It's the emotional attachment that forms when an abuser alternates cruelty with affection, creating confusion, dependency, and hope. It is not about enabling—it's about survival.

Trauma Bonding vs Codependency

Category	Trauma Bonding	Codependency
Root Cause	Abuse, coercive control, intermittent reinforcement	Learned roles and relational dysfunction, often from childhood
Emotional Dynamics	Confusion, fear, hope, emotional entrapment	Guilt, anxiety, compulsive caretaking
Behavioral Motivation	Survival, trying to avoid punishment or earn love	Desire to feel needed or in control
Typical Environment	Abusive or coercively controlling relationship	Mutual dysfunction; not necessarily abusive
Role of Abuse	Central to the dynamic; creates the bond	May be present, but not central or defining
Freedom to Leave	Limited or manipulated; often believes God wants her to stay	Typically able to leave, but feels responsible
Core Emotion	Fear	Guilt
Healing Approach	Safety, truth, trauma recovery, spiritual clarity	Boundaries, detachment, emotional independence

Mislabeling Hurts

When women are told they're codependent, they're often given advice like:

"You need to stop enabling."

"You're choosing to stay because you want to feel needed."

"You're addicted to helping him."

This advice can feel deeply shaming—and it misses the mark. Many of the women I've spoken with were not staying because they felt needed. They stayed because they were afraid. Because they were spiritually manipulated. Because they were trauma bonded. Because they believed God wanted them to keep their marriage vows no matter what. They stayed because they were holding out hope that the person their husband once *pretended* to be might reappear if they just prayed harder, sacrificed more, or kept the faith. They also have trouble seeing themselves as victims because they have been blamed for the abuse repeatedly.

That's not codependency. That's *abuse.*

The Heart of the Confusion

The confusion often lies in how outward behavior can look the same in both dynamics: over functioning, rescuing, walking on eggshells, caretaking, or sacrificing needs. But the motivation and context are different:

- In codependency, these behaviors often arise from a need to be needed or a desire to feel in control.

- In trauma bonding, these behaviors often arise from fear, manipulation, coercion, or spiritual distortion of biblical principles.

Leslie Vernick speaks directly to this dynamic:

"When you give another person the power to define you, then you also give them the power to control you."[ix]

Women in trauma bonds have often surrendered their identity, not because they want to be controlled—but because they've been trained through fear and false doctrine to believe that their self-sacrifice is holy. It isn't. It's harmful.

A Biblical Lens

Scripture calls us to love sacrificially but not to be enslaved to harm. Jesus never commanded us to stay bound to sin, deception, or abuse under the guise of loyalty or "faithfulness." Trauma bonding is not faithfulness. It is bondage. And the One who came to set captives free does not shame women for being trapped in it.

When we call trauma bonding what it is, we open the door to real healing. We remove the shame of being mislabeled. We affirm the woman's dignity, wisdom, and capacity to see clearly once the fog lifts.

And we remind her: staying in an abusive relationship doesn't mean she's codependent. It means she's been harmed— and that harm has a name. So does healing.

A Steady Love in the Midst of Chaos

The emotional chaos of intermittent reinforcement can feel like love—but it's a counterfeit. Real love doesn't leave you guessing. God's love is not manipulative. It doesn't swing wildly from cruelty to kindness. Scripture describes His character over and over with words like *faithful, steadfast, unchanging.*

> "*I have loved you with an everlasting love; I have drawn you with unfailing kindness.*"
>
> Jeremiah 31:3

This is the kind of love your heart was made for—not one that keeps you emotionally starved and then feeds you crumbs to keep you coming back. God's love doesn't leave you anxious, confused, or unsafe. It casts out fear (1 John 4:18). It is consistent, clear, and rooted in truth.

When Jesus described the thief in John 10:10, He said the thief comes only to "*steal and kill and destroy.*" But He came so that we might have life—and life to the full. The cycle of abuse robs you of that fullness. It trains you to survive on less, to call chaos "passion," and to confuse apology with repentance. It convinces you that your suffering is proof of loyalty or faith instead of a red flag that something is deeply broken.

You are not called to live on edge, hoping your husband's next good moment will be the real one. You are called to peace. To wisdom. To discernment. To the kind of love that reflects Christ—one that does not harm under the guise of spiritual growth.

Chapter 9 Discussion Questions –

1. **"Why Do I Still Feel Afraid?"**
   Sarah's question is one many women ask silently. Have you experienced fear or confusion even after your partner became sober? What are the signs that something deeper than addiction may still be harming you?

2. **Craving the Highs**
   Have you noticed yourself clinging to the "good moments" as evidence that change is happening? What emotional cost are you paying to hold on to those highs?

3. **Spiritual Bait**
   Has Scripture ever been used to pressure you into staying in a harmful situation? How has spiritual language blurred your sense of what is truly loving, safe, or godly?

4. **Church Applause, Private Pain**
   Like Lisa, have you ever felt invisible or dismissed because others celebrated your partner's recovery? What damage has that done to your voice, clarity, or sense of truth?

5. **Trauma Bonding vs. Codependency**

   Were you ever told you were codependent when you were actually experiencing trauma bonding? How did that label affect your understanding of yourself?

6. **Are You Living on Crumbs?**

   What does emotional "bread" look like to you? Have you been surviving on crumbs—occasional affection, praise, or apologies—hoping they'll eventually add up to love?

7. **Survival or Submission?**

   Have you mistaken your trauma responses (overfunctioning, silence, caretaking) for godly submission or faithfulness? What would a clearer, healthier picture of biblical love look like?

8. **God's Love vs. Emotional Chaos**

   How does God's love—described as *everlasting, unfailing, and faithful*—differ from the love you're experiencing at home? What does that difference tell you?

Chapter 10:

TACTICS OF A TOXIC PERSON

A person who has been in life-dominating addiction is a master of manipulation, regardless of who they are. That does not mean that all people who have a history of addiction continue in those patterns; however, in the case of those who claim to be set free but continue to live a life of abuse and coercive control of their partner, manipulation tactics are extremely well-developed skills that have carried over into their relationships post active addiction.

The following are common manipulation tactics used in toxic relationships:

Psychological Manipulation Tactics

1. Gaslighting—Making you doubt your reality or memory.
2. Blame-Shifting—Turning the blame onto you instead of taking responsibility.

3. Projection—Accusing you of behaviors or feelings they themselves exhibit.

4. Triangulation—Bringing in a third party to create drama or doubt.

5. Silent Treatment—Withholding communication as a form of control.

6. Love Bombing—Overwhelming with affection to gain control (usually intermittent).

7. Guilt-Tripping—Making you feel guilty for their actions or feelings.

8. Shaming—Making you feel inadequate or unworthy.

9. Playing the Victim—Always portraying themselves as the wronged party.

10. Minimization—Dismissing or downplaying your feelings and concerns.

11. DARVO—The Manipulator's Favorite Defense Play. Because this tactic is used so frequently, we will spend some time on this concept.

DARVO stands for Deny, Attack, Reverse Victim and Offender. It is one of the most common manipulation tactics that an abusive person will use to try to control you. If you confront them about something they have said or done, they will deny that it happened or they will attack you as being critical, unforgiving, mean, or whatever else they can say that would hurt you. Reverse victim and offender is to try to make you look like the one who has done something wrong to them so that you will not hold them accountable for anything. They will often go from one part of DARVO to another within minutes. If one thing isn't working, they can change course so fast that it makes your head spin! This is especially common in spiritually abusive or post-addiction contexts—where a person may have a convincing testimony, a well-practiced language of repentance, or the ability to "cry on cue" when confronted.

It's a psychological and spiritual maneuver designed to flip the script—so the one doing harm becomes the one *claiming* harm, and the one asking for accountability is recast as the *villain*. It could also be called "**crazy-making**," as it is hard to tell reality from their manipulation.

Deny

The first step in DARVO is to deny the abuse altogether. This can range from flat-out denial—"That never happened"—to subtle reframing that makes you seem overly sensitive or even spiritually deceived.

"That's not what I meant—you're twisting my words."

"I don't remember it that way. Maybe you need to pray about why this is bothering you so much."

When a spiritually manipulative person denies wrongdoing, it's often paired with Christian language that makes *you* feel like the problem. Suddenly, the issue isn't their behavior—it's your unforgiveness, your emotional instability, or your supposed spiritual blindness.

Attack

Next, the abuser pivots from defense to offense. You are no longer simply mistaken—you are dangerous. Accusations fly, often cloaked in moral or biblical terms.

"You're bitter and divisive. That's not from God."

"You're tearing down a man of God who's trying to change."

"You're disrespecting spiritual authority and grieving the Holy Spirit."

This stage is especially painful for women of faith, because it targets their deepest desire: to be godly, to walk in humility, to do the right thing. The attack is meant to disarm—to make you feel too ashamed or too uncertain to keep speaking.

Reverse Victim and Offender

The final blow comes when the toxic person rewrites the narrative so they become the "true" victim. They may cry, talk about spiritual warfare, or share just enough of their own brokenness to win sympathy—from you, the church, or anyone watching.

"I've been doing so much soul work, and now I'm being attacked."

"You're trying to ruin my testimony."

"People don't realize how hard it is for me—and now even my own wife is against me."

If he's in recovery, he may say things like, "*After all I've overcome, I don't deserve this.*" Or "*I'm trying to be a godly man—you just want me to fail.*"

The truth is buried under emotion and performance. And if he has a history of addiction, his recovery story becomes a shield—used to silence anyone who dares suggest he hasn't changed as much as he claims.

DARVO and the Church

In faith communities, DARVO can be especially toxic because it often *works*. Church leaders may see only the tears, hear the confessions, or be swayed by the public image of a "changed man." The real victim may be labeled as critical, unforgiving, or rebellious—especially if she refuses to keep quiet.

This is one of the most common patterns I hear from women whose husbands are no longer drinking or using drugs—but who are still controlling, cruel, or manipulative behind closed doors. The community celebrates the sobriety. The "big testimony" becomes untouchable. And any challenge to that narrative is met with DARVO.

Emily: A Story of DARVO in Action
Emily thought things were finally getting better.
After years of chaotic drinking and drug use, her husband, Jake, had gone to a well-known Christian recovery program. He came back with a testimony that brought the whole church to

tears—how God had broken him, how he had surrendered, how he was now "a new creation." He gave his life to Jesus, started attending men's group, and was invited to share his story at local churches and recovery events.

But at home, the charm wore off quickly.

Jake was no longer drinking—but he was still exploding in rage if Emily disagreed with him. He criticized how she prayed, how she disciplined the kids, even how she folded towels. When she tried to bring it up gently, he'd accuse her of "being led by a spirit of rebellion." Once, when she asked him not to yell in front of the kids, he shouted, "You're attacking my authority! You're out of order, and God's going to deal with you!"

When she finally reached out to their pastor's wife for help, Jake found out and launched into full DARVO mode.

Deny: "I never said that. She always twists everything I say."

Attack: "She's the one who's manipulative. She's disrespectful and cold—and she doesn't support me as the spiritual leader."

Reverse Victim and Offender: "I'm trying so hard to walk with the Lord and she's tearing me down. Why can't she just forgive and move on? I've changed. I'm not the same man. She just wants me to be the bad guy forever."

The pastor's wife told Emily she might be struggling with bitterness. "You need to let the past stay in the past," she said kindly. "Jake's sober now. He's walking with God. Maybe you need to trust God to change your heart."

Emily left that conversation more confused and ashamed than ever. She had watched her husband use the language of recovery and redemption to build a reputation—and now he was using it to shield himself from accountability. Worse, he had twisted her longing for peace and safety into a "sin issue."

She wasn't bitter. She was scared.

She wasn't unforgiving. She was exhausted.

But DARVO had done its job. He was the one getting hugs and prayers. She was left alone with the reality behind the testimony.

Control and Domination Tactics

1. Financial Control—Restricting access to money to limit independence.
2. Isolating—Cutting you off from friends and family.
3. Threatening—Using intimidation or implied threats to keep control.
4. Constant Criticism—Undermining your confidence with relentless negativity.
5. Boundary Violation—Disrespecting or ignoring your personal limits.
6. Intimidation—Using aggressive behavior to make you feel afraid.
7. Excessive Monitoring—Controlling your actions, whereabouts, or communications.

Deception and Exploitation Tactics

1. Lying—Twisting the truth or making false statements.

2. Withholding Information—Keeping details from you to maintain an upper hand.

3. Future Faking—Making false promises about the future to keep you invested.

4. Double Standards—Having different rules for themselves than for you.

5. Grooming—Gradually breaking down your defenses over time.

6. Feigning Ignorance—Pretending not to understand to avoid accountability.

7. Pathological Lying—Lying compulsively, even about unnecessary things.

8. Gaslighting—Attempting to make someone doubt their sanity.

Here are some religious/spiritual manipulation tactics that toxic individuals use to control or exploit others:

Religious/Spiritual Manipulation Tactics

1. Weaponizing Faith—Using religious teachings to justify control, abuse, or toxic behavior.

2. Shame-Based Control—Convincing others that they are sinful, impure, or unworthy unless they obey.

3. Selective Scripture Use—Quoting religious texts out of context to manipulate or coerce behavior.

4. Claiming Divine Authority—Saying they have a special connection to God/spirituality to demand obedience.

5. Demonizing Dissent—Labeling disagreement as rebellion against God or faith.

6. Fear of Divine Punishment—Threatening hell, bad consequences, or curses for disobedience.

7. Spiritual Gaslighting—Making someone question their own faith, spiritual experiences, or worthiness.

8. Forced Forgiveness—Insisting that the victim forgive and reconcile while ignoring accountability.

9. Holier-Than-Thou Attitude—Acting spiritually superior to belittle or control others.

10. Guilt-Tripping Through Faith—Using religious obligations to make someone feel guilty or indebted.

11. Exclusion & Isolation—Cutting off those who don't conform to religious expectations.

12. Prosperity Gospel Manipulation—Teaching that suffering is due to a lack of faith or financial giving.

13. Cults & Groupthink—Demanding blind loyalty to a leader or group while discouraging critical thinking.

14. Spiritual Bypassing—Using faith to dismiss real problems (e.g., "Just pray about it" instead of taking action).

15. False Prophecy & Visions—Claiming divine messages to manipulate decisions or actions.

Perhaps the most devastating kind of manipulation is the spiritual kind—when faith, Scripture, or God himself is used to keep someone trapped. This is particularly painful for women who truly want to honor God and live faithfully but are told that their suffering is somehow holy or deserved.

- Quoting Scripture selectively to justify sin or silence you.
- Telling you that disagreeing with them means rebelling against God.
- Claiming divine authority or "spiritual headship" in order to dominate.
- Using spiritual jargon to avoid responsibility: "God told me to do this" or "You're under spiritual attack."
- Demanding instant forgiveness while refusing repentance or change.
- Pressuring you to submit, stay, or stay silent in the name of being Christlike.

Spiritual manipulation turns the very thing that should set you free—your relationship with God—into a cage. But God is not the author of confusion or coercion. He is the God of truth, clarity, and freedom.

Overt, Covert, and Physical Tactics of a Toxic Person

Toxic people rarely rely on just one kind of manipulation—they often use a combination of emotional, spiritual, physical, and psychological tactics, adapting them based on what gets the most control with the least resistance. What makes many of these tactics so painful is how subtle they can be, especially in

Christian settings where "niceness," submission, and forgiveness are often elevated above truth and safety. Recognizing these patterns is the first step toward reclaiming your sense of reality.

Overt Abuse Tactics: The Obvious Ones

Overt abuse is loud. It's easy to name because it's visible, often explosive, and hard to deny. These behaviors are direct assaults on your dignity and safety.

- Yelling, name-calling, or using cruel language.
- Physical intimidation—getting in your face, slamming doors, punching walls, threatening gestures.
- Threatening harm or destruction.
- Shaming you in public or private.
- Controlling your movements, money, or relationships.
- Demanding obedience while citing Scripture as proof of their "authority."

When these kinds of behaviors happen, you *know* something's wrong. They're not hidden—they're just terrifying. The damage is immediate and intense.

Covert Abuse Tactics: The Hidden Ones

Covert abuse is quieter—but often more damaging in the long run. These tactics are designed to confuse you, make you question yourself, and slowly dismantle your confidence. They don't always "look" like abuse, especially from someone who knows how to play the victim or wear the mask of the godly spouse.

- Gaslighting: "That never happened. You're just too emotional."
- Guilt-tripping, especially with spiritual overtones.
- Passive-aggressive behavior that keeps you off balance.
- Triangulating—bringing other people into the situation to shame, confuse, or isolate you.
- Emotional withdrawal: punishing you with silence or indifference while still looking like the "good guy" to everyone else.
- Pretending to misunderstand, play dumb, or forget your boundaries on repeat.

Covert abuse thrives in Christian spaces because it's easy to hide behind verses, smiles, and a good testimony. But the confusion it creates is real—and its goal is the same: control.

Physical Tactics: Control Through Force or Fear

Not every toxic person is physically abusive—but when physical tactics *are* present, they're almost always part of a larger system of control. And physical abuse isn't limited to visible bruises or broken bones—it includes anything that uses the body, space, or physical power to dominate.

- Hitting, shoving, grabbing, choking, or restraining.
- Blocking exits, cornering you during arguments.
- Destroying objects or throwing things to intimidate.
- Using physical size or proximity to make you feel unsafe.
- Forcing sexual activity, especially under the guise of "marital duty."
- Controlling sleep, food, or basic needs.

The message behind physical tactics is simple: *You are not safe, and I am in control.* Whether the abuse leaves bruises or not, it leaves a mark. Sometimes it only happens rarely or even once. The message is clear: he is willing and able to use force to control and intimidate you. He teaches you well to fear him.

Chapter 10 Discussion Questions

1. **What Are You Afraid Of?**
   If you imagine walking away from the abuse, what specific fears rise to the surface? Are they emotional,

spiritual, financial, or relational? How might those fears be keeping you frozen?

2. **False Guilt vs. Godly Conviction**

   What guilt are you carrying that may not be from God? How can you tell the difference between Holy Spirit conviction and the shame that keeps you stuck?

3. **"God Hates Divorce"—or Does He Hate Abuse More?**

   Have you ever been told that staying is your spiritual duty? How does that belief hold up when placed next to God's character of justice, mercy, and protection for the oppressed?

4. **Biblical Boundaries: Permission or Punishment?**

   When you try to set boundaries, what kind of pushback do you receive—from your partner, your church, or even yourself? What does Scripture actually say about boundaries and wisdom?

5. **Overfunctioning and the Savior Complex**

   Are you doing all the emotional, spiritual, or even practical labor in the relationship? In what ways have you taken responsibility for things that are not yours to carry?

6. **Identity Theft**

   Abuse distorts identity. What lies about yourself have you started to believe? What truths about your worth and value does God speak over you instead?

7. **Breaking Free: What Does Freedom *Actually* Look Like?**

   If you could define freedom—not in vague terms, but

in practical, daily life—what would it look like for you? What is one small step you can take toward that today?

8. **Permission to Want Peace**

   Do you feel guilty for wanting peace, rest, and emotional safety? Why? Who told you that wanting peace was selfish—and what might God say in response?

Chapter 11:

MYTHS THAT KEEP WOMEN TRAPPED

Introduction: Unmasking the Myths That Keep Women Trapped

Abuse doesn't always wear a black eye or show up with police reports. In Christian communities, it often hides behind misused Scripture, pious-sounding advice, and cultural expectations about marriage. Women are told to endure, to sacrifice, to submit—no matter what. They are taught that keeping a marriage intact is always more righteous than confronting the sin that's destroying it from the inside out.

The most dangerous lies are the ones that sound almost true. They slip into sermons, books, and counseling sessions as unquestioned wisdom. They shape how women understand their role, their suffering, and even the character of God. These myths don't just cause confusion—they cause captivity.

In the following pages, we'll expose some of the most common and harmful beliefs that keep women trapped in emotionally, spiritually, and sometimes physically abusive marriages. With each myth, we'll offer not only clarity and truth but also a vision of a God who does not require His daughters to stay in chains for the sake of appearances. The truth sets us free—and it begins by naming the lies.

Myth #1: "A woman needs to submit more and give him more sex so he will stop mistreating her"

This myth is often rooted in a distorted interpretation of Scripture and a toxic view of marriage that places all the burden on the wife to fix what's broken. Women are told that if they were more submissive, more sexually available, more agreeable, or more respectful, their husbands would be kinder, more loving, and less angry. The message is clear: if your husband is mistreating you, it's probably your fault.

This belief weaponizes biblical concepts like submission and intimacy, turning them into tools of coercion rather than expressions of mutual love. It reinforces the false idea that women are responsible for managing their husband's behavior—spiritually, emotionally, and sexually. But submission was never meant to require enduring abuse. And sex was never intended to be a duty performed under pressure, fear, or obligation.

In *The Great Sex Rescue*, Sheila Wray Gregoire dismantles this harmful teaching by exposing the damage it causes: "When women are told their bodies belong to their husbands, and that refusing sex is a sin, it sets the stage for coercion, not connection. That is not God's design for intimacy."[x]

Participating in sin is not honoring God—either by committing it or by enabling it. If a husband is sinning against his wife—emotionally, sexually, or spiritually—her compliance or silence will not sanctify him but will only allow the abuse to continue and get worse.

Psalm 82 Initiative, in a Facebook post on 7/15/24, says it well:

"By suggesting that a woman can 'change' her abusive husband by adjusting her behavior and being more submissive, you are doing two things...

1. You are requiring the wife to be the spiritual leader, while demanding that they pretend that the husband is the leader.
2. You are undermining the husband's autonomy and telling him that he is helpless to control his own thoughts, feelings, and actions."

Andrew Bauman said "we cannot normalize toxic masculinity, sexism, or abusive behavior. That is not how men act; that is how young boys behave."[xi]

God's design for marriage is mutual love, honor, and sacrifice—not control, manipulation, or sexual entitlement. A woman is not her husband's sanctification project or his emotional regulator. She is his equal partner, fully made in the image of God, deserving of respect, protection, and love.

Myth #2: "God hates divorce"—therefore, you must stay

"God hates divorce" is one of the most quoted phrases in Christian circles—often used to silence women who are in abusive marriages. The implication is that no matter what is happening behind closed doors, leaving is never an option because it would displease God. But this phrase is built on a mistranslation and a misrepresentation of God's heart.

The actual Hebrew in Malachi 2:16 is difficult to translate, but many modern scholars now recognize that the passage likely says something closer to: "The man who hates and divorces his wife does violence to the one he should protect." The emphasis is not that God hates all divorce—it's that He hates treachery, betrayal, and violence in marriage.

God does not hate all divorce. He does, however, hate the violation of covenant love and the cruelty that makes it necessary for people to escape. He hates when people are kept in chains on the basis of His name.

God's plan for His daughters was never to remain in marriages marked by abuse, oppression, or betrayal. Just as He freed the Israelites from slavery, He sees and rescues women today. He is the same God.

When we read the whole counsel of Scripture, we see a God who is not legalistic but loving, a God who prioritizes the protection of the vulnerable over the preservation of appearances. Divorce is not God's ideal—but neither is abuse, treachery, or the slow destruction of a woman's soul.

Using "God hates divorce" as a blanket command to stay in all situations—no matter the harm—is not only a misuse of Scripture but also a misrepresentation of the character of God. The God of the Bible does not require women to sacrifice their safety or sanity to preserve a covenant that has already been broken by chronic sin.

Myth #3: "If he didn't hit you, it's not abuse"

Many women in the church have been told, or have silently internalized, the dangerous belief that unless their husbands are hitting them, what they're experiencing doesn't "count" as abuse. This myth has allowed countless abusive dynamics to go unnoticed, unchallenged, and even defended by church leaders. But emotional, psychological, and spiritual abuse are not lesser forms of harm. In fact, they often leave deeper wounds than bruises.

Abuse is the crushing of God's image. Silence, words, coercive control, and humiliation can be used to diminish and destroy a person. The Church must develop eyes to see beyond the lack of visible bruises to the destruction inside.

Author and survivor advocate Natalie Hoffman echoes this reality, describing emotional abuse as "death by a thousand cuts."[xii] In her book *Is It Me?*, she explains how women often doubt themselves because the abuse they endure is covert—laced with gaslighting, blame-shifting, and spiritual manipulation. Hoffman helps women recognize the patterns of control that can entrap them even in the absence of visible violence.

Sheila Wray Gregoire also points to the way toxic marriage advice can mask abuse. Her research-based book *The Great Sex Rescue* challenges teachings that tell women their role is to keep their husbands sexually satisfied no matter how they're being treated. "When you are told that your body does not belong to you," Gregoire writes, "you are no longer seen as a person with agency. That is the foundation of abuse."[xiii]

Gretchen Baskerville names the problem plainly: "You don't have to be physically beaten to be in a destructive marriage. Chronic emotional cruelty is soul-damaging."[xiv] She shares stories of Christian women who stayed for years in harmful marriages because they were told that unless they could prove bruises, they had no biblical right to leave.

Sarah McDugal, who specializes in helping Christian women escape coercive control, warns that too many churches ignore red flags unless the abuse turns criminal. She writes, "Coercive control is the foundation of all abuse. Physical violence is simply one of its symptoms."[xv] She calls on the Church to stop minimizing psychological harm and begin protecting the vulnerable.

This myth has left women spiritually silenced and emotionally crushed. As Christ's body, we are called to expose it—and stand fiercely with the unseen, unheard, and unprotected.

Myth #4: "You're not here to be happy. You're here to be holy."

This phrase has been repeated so often in Christian marriage circles that it's treated like Scripture itself. The message is clear: God cares more about your spiritual growth than your emotional or physical well-being, and if you're suffering in your marriage, it's likely part of His sanctifying plan. But this myth is often weaponized to keep people, especially women, in damaging and dangerous marriages.

Yes, God does care about holiness. But holiness in Scripture is never developed through enabling sin or enduring abuse. Holiness means being set apart for God's purposes, and it includes living in truth, love, and freedom. Enduring cruelty is not the path to righteousness; partnering with destructive patterns is not sanctification.

As Sheila Wray Gregoire teaches, we aren't called to sacrifice ourselves on the altar of marriage. Enabling sin doesn't develop holiness.

What's often missed in this conversation is that God cares deeply about justice, mercy, and compassion. The idea that God is pleased with a woman suffering indefinitely under coercion, control, or emotional neglect contradicts His heart revealed throughout Scripture. Jesus did not call the oppressed to suffer silently so others could stay comfortable in their sin. He came to set captives free (John 10:10).

Framing abuse as part of one's sanctification can spiritually paralyze victims, making them feel they are betraying God by leaving. But Scripture does not tell women to sacrifice their God-given dignity and safety on the altar of someone else's unchecked sin. True holiness includes truth, courage, and sometimes walking away from evil.

This myth keeps too many trapped in marriages that destroy their health, joy, and even their faith. It must be exposed for what it is: spiritual distortion. God doesn't call us to marriages that slowly kill our souls. He calls us to walk in the light, in truth, and in love—and sometimes that means walking away.

Lysa TerKeurst, on the podcast Therapy and Theology, said "Jesus laid down His Life for a high and holy purpose, not to enable bad behavior."

Luke 4:18 says, "*The spirit of the Lord is on me, because he has anointed me to proclaim good news to the poor. He has sent me to proclaim freedom for the prisoners and recovery of sight for the blind, to set the oppressed free.*"

Myth #5: "Children are better off with two parents, no matter what"

One of the most persistent and damaging myths in Christian communities is the belief that children are always better off in a two-parent home—even if one parent is abusive. Women are told to "stay for the kids," "hang on until they're grown," or "keep the family together at all costs." But what is the real cost of staying in a home filled with fear, tension, and emotional chaos?

Research tells a very different story. Children who grow up in abusive environments—whether the abuse is directed at them or witnessed in the treatment of their mother—often suffer long-term psychological, emotional, and even physical consequences. Chronic exposure to domestic abuse has been linked to anxiety, depression, PTSD, poor academic performance, and increased likelihood of perpetuating or entering into abusive relationships themselves. In short, staying "for the kids" often harms them more than it helps.

Gretchen Baskerville challenges this myth, pointing out that toxic homes teach children that "love" looks like contempt, chaos, and fighting. She cites studies that show children often thrive after a divorce that removes them from an abusive situation—especially when the remaining parent is stable, safe, and emotionally healthy.

Spiritual harm done is done to children who watch abuse being tolerated or excused in the name of faith. Children form their concept of God by watching what the adults in their life do, not just what they say, and will believe that God approves of abuse by seeing the way their mother is mistreated under the guise of submission.

When the Church upholds the idol of marriage above the well-being of those inside it, it sends a dangerous message to both adults and children: that appearances matter more than truth, and that suffering in silence is a virtue. But Scripture paints a different picture. God is a refuge for the oppressed. He defends the vulnerable. He invites the broken into healing.

Keeping children in an abusive household does not protect them—it exposes them. And it teaches them a distorted view of love, safety, and even God. Telling women to stay "for the children" is not only misguided; it is often a form of spiritual and emotional abuse in itself. Sometimes, the holiest, most loving thing a mother can do is to remove her children from a harmful environment and choose safety over appearances.

Myth #6: "Most divorces are frivolous, even in the church community"

This myth persists both inside and outside the Church: that most divorces—especially among Christians—are impulsive, selfish, or rooted in shallow reasons. People assume couples are simply "giving up" because they're unhappy, bored, or unwilling to sacrifice. The implication is clear: most divorces are morally suspect, and those who choose them are spiritually immature.

But this assumption doesn't hold up to either the data or the lived experience of countless women in abusive marriages.

The truth is that the majority of divorces among Christian women—especially those initiated after years of suffering—are not frivolous at all. They are often heartbreaking, last-resort decisions made in the face of chronic mistreatment, emotional abandonment, betrayal, coercion, and even ongoing danger. Many women who finally choose to leave have spent years begging for change, pleading with pastors for help, enduring counseling sessions that minimized their pain, and praying for a miracle that never came. Divorce, for them, is not a whim—it is survival.

Gretchen Baskerville confronts this myth directly. She shares data from her research showing that a large percentage of divorces—especially those classified as "life-saving"—stem from serious issues like abuse, addiction, infidelity, and chronic neglect. "The idea that Christians divorce over petty irritations is simply false," she writes. "Most women stay too long, not too little."[xvi]

Sadly, this myth has been used to shame survivors and silence their stories. Women who have endured years of emotional harm are met with suspicion, told they should have prayed harder, or accused of breaking their vows—while the destructive behavior of their husbands is downplayed or ignored. The church often becomes an unsafe place, compounding their trauma.

It's time to shift the narrative. Not all divorces are created equal. Some are selfish, yes—but many are sacred acts of courage in the face of evil. Many are the result of choosing life, dignity, and healing after long seasons of despair. These are not "easy outs"; they are hard-won escapes from harm.

As people of faith, we are called to speak truth and extend compassion—not blanket condemnation. Blanket statements about divorce overlook the complexity of abuse, addiction, trauma, and survival. Jesus met people in their pain and saw their stories. We must do the same.

Myth #7: "People still end up unhappy after the divorce"

This myth suggests that divorce is a guaranteed path to lifelong sadness, regret, and dysfunction. Many women are told or fear that if they choose to end their marriage, they will forever carry the weight of failure, bitterness, or a lack of fulfillment. The implication is that leaving an abusive or unhealthy marriage will only lead to a future of emotional ruin, loneliness, or missed opportunities for true happiness. It's a myth that paints divorce as the ultimate tragedy, suggesting that no matter the circumstances, separation only leads to sorrow.

The reality, however, is much more complex. Divorce, especially in cases of abuse or chronic emotional neglect, can be the first step toward healing, wholeness, and new beginnings. While divorce can bring significant emotional challenges—grief over the loss of a relationship, the shattering of dreams, and the changes in family dynamics—many women find that once free from an abusive or controlling partner, they experience an overwhelming sense of relief, empowerment, and renewed purpose.

According to studies, divorce does not sentence a person to a life of misery. Many women, after leaving an abusive marriage, find joy again in discovering their identity outside the confines of abuse. They regain control over their lives, rediscover passions and gifts that were suppressed or ignored, and begin to thrive in a healthy, supportive environment. Divorce can open doors to emotional and spiritual healing that may have seemed impossible when trapped in a controlling relationship.

Staying in a destructive relationship causes deep soul wounds; it is not possible to heal while in the situation in which one is being harmed. Many survivors report finding peace, strength, and fulfillment after they leave, not because the process is easy, but because it allows them to reclaim their lives.

Another important aspect of this myth is the assumption that happiness is always defined by marriage or romantic relationship status. For many women, the pursuit of happiness is about safety, peace, and the freedom to be themselves—none of which are guaranteed or even possible in an abusive marriage. Women who have left toxic relationships often find that, without the constant threat or manipulation of an abusive spouse, they are better able to focus on their well-being, build healthier relationships with friends and family, and develop a sense of inner peace that was impossible before.

Furthermore, research indicates that, for many people who have experienced abuse, staying in the marriage actually increases emotional and psychological distress. According to studies cited by Sarah McDugal (Wilderness to Wild), those who leave abusive marriages often experience a sharp decline in anxiety, depression, and post-traumatic stress symptoms once they are no longer in the abusive environment. Divorce can offer freedom and relief—particularly when staying would mean continuing to endure harm.

It's important to recognize that divorce itself is not the cause of ongoing unhappiness, but rather, it's the toxic dynamics of an abusive relationship that breed emotional suffering. Leaving an abusive marriage does not guarantee immediate happiness, especially if there is ongoing contact with the abuser due to child custody issues, but it offers the possibility of healing, self-discovery, and a life free from ongoing trauma.

The church, however, has often perpetuated the myth that divorce leads only to lasting sadness, using it as a means of guilt-tripping women back into harmful marriages. This myth further isolates those who have chosen divorce, making them feel as though they have failed in their pursuit of holiness. In fact, some in the church have acted throughout history as if divorce is the unpardonable sin. Yet, the true path to healing often begins with the difficult but necessary step of leaving an unhealthy relationship.

What many women discover in the aftermath of divorce is that they can build a fulfilling life—one rooted in self-respect, dignity, and peace. They can experience happiness that was previously elusive, not because of their marital status, but because they have reclaimed control of their lives and chosen safety and health over enduring harm.

In summary, the myth that divorce leads only to lifelong unhappiness disregards the very real healing and growth that can take place after leaving an abusive marriage. True happiness does not come from staying in a relationship for the sake of appearances or duty; it comes from the freedom to live without fear, to thrive without manipulation, and to choose life over survival.

Myth #8: "It takes two to tango"—both people are responsible for the problems

Tango

"It takes two to have a good relationship, but it only takes one to destroy it. Read that again. A common comment is that it takes two to tango. Actually, no it doesn't. It takes two for a good tango, but it only takes one to not participate that ruins the dance.

You go out on the dance floor with every intention of doing your part in the dance. You stand there with your partner waiting with great anticipation for the music to start. The music starts and as you go to start the dance your partner sits on the floor refusing to move. You believe you only get one chance for this dance, so you drag him all over the dance floor. You are now taking on not only your part of the dance but carrying his dead weight as well. He yells and criticizes you for not making the dance look great, so you do more and try harder to make this dance look good. The less he does the more you do. The more you do the less he does. You wonder why this dance is so hard. This dance should not be this hard! Why is it so hard?!

You look around the dance floor and see others looking great dancing around like they are supposed to. You then think, "What am I doing wrong that we aren't dancing like that. You know the dance and you are doing your part so why is it so hard and exhausting? Why do others glide around the dance floor making this look so effortless? You then ask them as they go dancing by what their secrets for a good dance are. They give you suggestions and tell you what you are doing wrong. You go back to your partner and try again and again and again. You think, "What am I doing wrong? I'm doing what others are doing in their successful dance so why isn't anything working for us? You've tried everything you know to, and it still isn't enough. But why?!

You let go of him and walk across the dancefloor looking for help. He is screaming at you to come back, putting you down for quitting and degrading you for doing such a poor job with the dance. Others are criticizing you and telling you to get back to dancing. It takes two to tango, right?! You doubt yourself. Others must know better, so you go back... time... and time... and time... again.

At some point you can't do this anymore. You are desperate. Nothing you do or try works. No matter what you do the dance isn't working and there isn't any more you can do. You've tried everything and then some. You are dazed, confused and disheartened. You are physically, emotionally, mentally and spiritually EXHAUSTED. Why are these things helping others around you to dance well but not you? You can't do this anymore. You let go of him to stand up straight, but you can't. Every muscle in your body is now cramped, sore and painful. Bending over and carrying his weight for so long your body doesn't know how to stand up straight anymore. You are now realizing the only thing left to do is get off the dancefloor and get help for yourself. The only thing you haven't done yet is to take care of you. The only way to take care of you is stop pulling his weight, doing his part of the dance and get off the dancefloor. You don't care anymore what he says or does or anyone else for that matter. You are desperate to save yourself.

You walk across the dancefloor in the midst of criticism, finger pointing and disparaging opinions of you. You know when you walk off that dancefloor you will be disqualified from the dance. That belief held you captive and made you a prisoner on the dancefloor. You don't care anymore, and you need out. Dancing the tango with him is destroying you. You walk off the dancefloor, see the exit sign and the first time in forever you have hope of fresh air and sunlight. You remember the days before you came to the auditorium to dance the tango on that dancefloor. The hope and excitement build the closer you get to the exit because you now remember the beauty, fresh air and safety on the other side of that door. You open the door to sunlight, fresh air and the hope of tomorrow as you take those steps toward healing and freedom."

– Terry Cooke (as quoted
by Brooklyn Masters).
Used by permission.

This phrase is often thrown out casually in marriage discussions, especially when someone tries to explain why their relationship is struggling or has ended. "Well, it takes two to tango," people say—as if every marital breakdown must be a 50/50 fault line. In fact, it was said to me by a well-respected person in my former church. In theory, this sounds fair. In practice, it often silences survivors of abuse and enables those who harm them.

This myth assumes that every conflict is mutual, that both people are equally to blame, and that if a marriage is broken, it's because both partners failed. But this is a deeply misleading—and in cases of abuse, harmful—assumption.

Yes, it takes two people to build a healthy marriage. It takes two to love well, communicate honestly, compromise, forgive, and grow. But it only takes **one** to destroy a relationship through control, manipulation, betrayal, or emotional violence. Just one person can unravel the safety, intimacy, and trust that a marriage depends on. It only takes one to destroy the dance.

Survivors are often pressured into owning part of the blame for the abuse they endured. They're asked, "What did you do to provoke him?" or "What part did you play in the breakdown of the marriage?" Even Christian counselors can perpetuate this myth, insisting that both partners need to "work on themselves" or "repent equally" when one partner is clearly violating the other's dignity and safety.

The other common phrase is that there are always two sides to every story. However, that implies that when a woman reports abuse, she may be slanting the story to make her husband look bad. While this can happen, it is much rarer than this phrase would imply. Usually, the woman has suffered in silence for a long time before speaking up. The root problem is not the marriage relationship; the problem is abuse.

When a spouse is being emotionally manipulated, lied to, gaslit, coerced, or chronically devalued, that is not a conflict—it's an offense. And repentance cannot be demanded from the victim to make the abuser feel justified.

Diane Langberg reminds us that evil often wears the mask of righteousness. Evil often seeks to cover itself by convincing others that both parties are equally at fault. This creates a false equivalency that shifts attention away from the real harm and burdens the victim with unjust guilt.

This myth is especially dangerous in the Church, where reconciliation is often prioritized over justice. When pastors or counselors treat all marital crises as mutual failures, they often force the victim into ongoing harm. Accountability gets diluted, and the abuser escapes both correction and consequence.

The truth is that many women have tried everything they could to make their marriage work. They've prayed, forgiven, submitted, gone to counseling, and sought advice. And still, the abuse continued. That is not a mutual failure. That is one person choosing to reject love, and another person surviving the consequences.

In a healthy marriage, yes—it takes two to tango. But in an abusive one, it only takes one to destroy the dance. And no one should be forced to keep dancing with someone who's kicking them off the floor.

Myth #9: "God sees divorce as a sin"

This myth is deeply embedded in many Christian communities—the idea that divorce, in and of itself, is inherently sinful. It's often implied or directly stated that no matter the circumstances, choosing divorce places someone outside God's will. As a result, women who leave abusive marriages are sometimes treated with suspicion or outright condemnation, as if they've fallen from grace simply by walking away from harm. In some churches, divorce is treated as the "unpardonable sin," forever defining her and limiting her from any kind of ministry or church leadership.

But Scripture does not teach that all divorce is sin. What it consistently condemns is betrayal, hardness of heart, treachery, and the breaking of covenant through selfishness, cruelty, or abandonment. The assumption that divorce is always a spiritual failure ignores both the complexity of human relationships and the compassionate character of God.

Divorce can be the result of sin—but it is not always a sin in itself. Sometimes it is the righteous response to sin. Sometimes it is the necessary path to healing and safety after years of mistreatment, neglect, or deceit. To call all divorce sinful is to place a crushing burden on the shoulders of those who have already suffered deeply.

Divorce often is just the legal ending of a covenant that was already broken before God.

The Bible contains numerous examples of God making room for separation when covenant has been violated. He divorced Israel (Jeremiah 3:8) when they persistently broke their covenant with Him. He provides for the protection of the vulnerable throughout both the Old and New Testaments. Jesus Himself condemned the hard-heartedness of those who treated divorce casually—not the person who walked away from injustice.

To say that all divorce is sin is to flatten the gospel into a legalistic rulebook and ignore the heart of God who sees, who grieves over injustice, and who calls His people to live in truth. Yes, divorce can be misused and done for selfish reasons. But it can also be done with trembling reverence, in the pursuit of peace and survival.

God does not stand over the shoulder of a battered, silenced woman and shame her for choosing to walk away from the one who has continually violated her soul. He stands beside her. He calls her beloved. He leads her out.

Myth #10: I Must be Loyal at all Cost "As Long as He Needs Me..."[xvii] — When Devotion Becomes a Chain

There's a cultural narrative that has long romanticized self-sacrificial love, especially from women. We've been taught that loyalty, no matter the cost, is a virtue. But when loyalty becomes a prison, it is no longer love—it is bondage.

Nowhere is this more heartbreakingly expressed than in the song "As Long As He Needs Me" from the musical *Oliver!*. Sung by Nancy, a woman who remains with her abuser out of a sense of twisted loyalty and longing, the lyrics echo the cry of countless women trapped in the cycle of abuse:

**"Who else would love him still,
When they've been used so ill?"**

**"As long as he needs me...
I know where I must be.
I'll cling on steadfastly...
As long as he needs me."**

Nancy isn't weak. She's loyal. She's committed. And she is completely and tragically trapped in the trauma bond of intermittent reinforcement—abused, minimized, discarded, and yet convinced that her loyalty will one day change him... or prove something righteous about her suffering. Her loyalty ultimately leads to her life tragically being cut short by her abuser.

Many Christian women in abusive relationships live in this same place. They've been told their highest calling is to be faithful—to love him through it all, to keep the covenant no matter what. They are urged to stay because "he needs you," or because "God hates divorce," or because "real love endures."

But the question is not *does he need me?* The real question is: **What does God say about covenant when one partner repeatedly breaks it through coercion, deception, and harm?**

Loyalty is a godly trait—when it's mutual, safe, and rightly placed. But when loyalty becomes complicity in your own destruction, it is no longer holy. It's hostage-taking disguised as devotion.

God never calls a woman to sustain abuse in the name of faithfulness. He calls us to truth, freedom, and dignity.

Summary and Scripture Reflection

These myths are not harmless misunderstandings—they are distortions that can keep women in chains. They excuse abuse, silence victims, and protect harmful systems rather than the people God loves. When these beliefs are allowed to stand unchallenged, they misrepresent the heart of God and leave the vulnerable unprotected.

But the truth is this: God does not call His daughters to endure abuse for the sake of appearances. He does not require silent suffering to prove holiness. He does not love the institution of marriage more than the individuals within it. And He never uses shame or fear to bind a woman to harm.

Scripture tells a different story—one of rescue, justice, and dignity. Psalm 34:18 says, *"The Lord is close to the brokenhearted and saves those who are crushed in spirit."* Isaiah 61 proclaims that God has come *"to bind up the brokenhearted, to proclaim freedom for the captives and release from darkness for the prisoners."*

Jesus Himself was not impressed with religious rules that oppressed the weak. He saw women others ignored. He spoke life where others imposed law. He silenced the accusers and lifted up the wounded. This is the God who still sees, still hears, and still delivers.

If you have believed these myths—or worse, if they have been used against you—know that the truth is stronger. You are not alone. God is not disappointed in your courage to seek safety and freedom. He is, in fact, already there calling you out of confusion and into His peace.

Chapter 11 Discussion Questions

1. **Which Myth Has Been Most Damaging to You?**
As you read through these ten myths, which one have you internalized the most—and how has it impacted your decisions, your faith, or your identity?

2. **Submission vs. Coercion**
Have you ever felt pressured to submit to or provide sex in order to avoid conflict or earn love? How does your view of biblical submission change when you consider mutuality and safety?

3. **The "God Hates Divorce" Narrative**
How has this phrase—often taken out of context—been used in your life or community? How does the truth about Malachi 2:16 reframe your understanding of God's heart?

4. **Defining Abuse Beyond Bruises**
Were you ever taught (directly or indirectly) that abuse had to be physical to "count"? How did that

shape your response to emotional or spiritual mistreatment?

5. **Holiness or Harm?**

Have you ever believed that staying in suffering was part of your sanctification? What would it look like to pursue holiness that includes truth, freedom, and emotional safety?

6. **"Staying for the Kids"**

What fears or hopes have shaped your choices about staying or leaving because of your children? How might your children be perceiving the relationship—and forming their own ideas about love and safety?

7. **Judging Others Who Leave**

Before your own experience, did you ever assume that most divorces were frivolous or selfish? How does hearing these myths challenged shift your judgment or compassion for others?

8. **Reclaiming Joy After Divorce**

Do you fear that you'll never be happy again if you leave? What are some areas where you've already seen glimpses of peace, relief, or hope—even if healing isn't complete?

9. **"It Takes Two" and False Guilt**

Have you been pressured to accept part of the blame for things your partner chose to do? What does it feel like to hear that one person's destructive behavior is *not* your responsibility?

10. **Misplaced Loyalty and Trauma Bonding**

Have you mistaken loyalty for love or faithfulness when it was really fear or trauma keeping you stuck? What would it mean to be loyal to *yourself* and to God's call to freedom?

Chapter 12:

CAN HE CHANGE? WILL HE CHANGE?

Introduction: The Hope and the Question

"He says he's sorry. Should I believe him?"
"He wants to come home. What if he's really different this time?"
"My pastor says I should forgive and give it another chance—especially for the kids."

For many women in abusive relationships—especially when addiction is part of the story—these questions hangs like a cloud over every decision: *Can he change? Will he?*

The answer is never easy, and the stakes feel impossibly high. In the Christian community, where forgiveness and reconciliation are held up as sacred goals, the pressure to believe in change is enormous. You may feel like the "godly" thing to do is to hope, to wait, to give it one more chance. Especially when your partner has quit drinking. Especially when he's finally going to church. Especially when he's crying, praying, quoting Scripture, or saying all the right things.

But hope, when untethered from reality, can become a trap. It is called "hopium," that strong desire for everything to be better that deludes our thinking and dulls our intuition.

Many women have walked this path—trying to trust that their partner's promises are real, only to find themselves right back in the same painful patterns: manipulation, entitlement, cruelty, coercion, spiritual abuse. Sometimes, the abuse even intensifies after a "conversion," because now he uses God's name to demand your compliance.

If you've found yourself asking, "*How do I know if he's really changed?*," you are not alone. And you are not faithless for asking. In fact, Scripture doesn't just allow discernment—it commands it.

This chapter is not here to tell you what to do. It's here to equip you with the clarity you need to make decisions in truth, not in confusion or fear. We'll explore the difference between true and false repentance, how to recognize patterns vs. fruit, and why you are not unbiblical for requiring more than empty words. You are not obligated to reconcile with someone who hasn't truly changed—no matter how many people are pressuring you to do so.

Let's start by looking at the difference between *change* and *charm*.

The Difference Between Change and Charm

Abusive men can be incredibly persuasive—especially when they feel like they're losing control. They might cry, pray, beg, apologize, and promise a new life. They may even go to counseling, join a recovery group, or memorize Bible verses.

A man stood before a men's breakfast at church and gave a testimony of how he had finally recognized that he had been coercing and punishing his wife for years. He loved the affirmations that came after his very moving talk. But that doesn't necessarily mean he changed (he hadn't).

In fact, many abusers are masters at looking repentant without actually repenting.

What's often mistaken for transformation is simply charm.

Charm is external. It's emotional. It's about managing appearances and manipulating outcomes. True change, by contrast, is internal. It's slow. It's painful. It's about humility, accountability, and surrendering control.

As Leslie Vernick wisely teaches, words alone are not repentance. True repentance is shown in changed behavior that is consistent over a long time. False repentance is sorrow over consequences—not over the harm caused. It's regret because he's uncomfortable or exposed, not because he's brokenhearted over his sin. His pain is because he got caught, not because he hurt you.

Even when there's an apology, it's often laced with manipulation:

- "I only acted that way because you pushed me."
- "I wouldn't have said that if you hadn't made me angry."
- "I'm sorry you feel that way."

These are not apologies. They're deflections. They place the blame on you and demand that your hurt be set aside so that he can be quickly restored.

Experts warn that one of the most difficult moments in an abusive dynamic is when the victim is persuaded to trust charm and regret instead of waiting for true repentance. The pressure to reconcile can be intense—not just from the abuser, but from pastors, counselors, and even family members who are uncomfortable with conflict or loss.

But reconciliation without transformation is not healing. It is another layer of harm. It is not unusual for a man to experience strong boundaries, including separation, and suddenly come across as deeply repentant, heartbroken, and willing to do whatever to get you to come home. They can use all the right terminology, consult with the pastor, agree to go to counseling, but once you give in and move back home, things usually get even worse than before after a brief "honeymoon" period. It is estimated that abused women leave an average of seven times before they finally say "enough." But you don't have to follow that pattern.

Jesus taught us to be wise as serpents and innocent as doves. He didn't say to be gullible or easily swayed by emotion. He told us to look for fruit. And fruit takes time to grow.

In the next section, we'll explore what true repentance looks like—and how to tell the difference between empty words and real change.

What True Repentance Actually Looks Like

Scripture gives us a clear picture of what real repentance is—and what it isn't.

II Corinthians 7:10–11 says,

> *"Godly sorrow brings repentance that leads to salvation and leaves no regret, but worldly sorrow brings death... See what this godly sorrow has produced in you: what earnestness, what eagerness to clear yourselves, what indignation, what alarm, what longing, what concern, what readiness to see justice done."*

Real repentance isn't just emotional. It's visible. It produces a deep desire to do what is right, to repair what was broken, and to accept the consequences—even when those consequences are hard.

In contrast, *worldly sorrow* often shows up as tears, regret, and apologies that come and go like the wind. It's a performance meant to smooth things over and quickly return to the way things were. But real repentance doesn't ask for a reset. It asks for transformation.

According to both the Psalm 82 Initiative (A Letter on Showing Repentance) and experts like Leslie Vernick, genuine repentance has consistent markers. Here's what it includes:

1. Taking Full Responsibility—Without Excuses

There is no blaming the victim, the addiction, the stress, or childhood wounds. A truly repentant person says, "*I did this. It was wrong. No one made me. I own it.*"

2. Accepting Consequences

A changed man doesn't demand restoration. He accepts that trust must be rebuilt slowly and may never fully return. He doesn't pressure his wife to reconcile or shame her for not being ready. He understands that consequences are not punishment— they are part of repentance.

3. Making Amends Without Expectations

True repentance seeks to repair damage done. Not to earn something back, but because it's the right thing to do. He may offer to pay for therapy, provide safety, or support the children consistently—not to win approval, but to take ownership.

4. Pursuing Long-Term Accountability

Real change doesn't happen in isolation. A repentant man welcomes outside input. He joins a serious program (not only a Bible study), submits to ongoing oversight, and makes his recovery transparent and verifiable. And he does this without being forced.

5. Bearing Long-Term Fruit

In Luke 3:8, John the Baptist said, *"Produce fruit in keeping with repentance."* That means change that shows up in daily life—not just during the honeymoon phase after a blow-up. True repentance isn't just about not doing bad things—it's about learning to do good, consistently, over time.

How He Handles Your "No"

One of the clearest indicators of real change in an abusive man—especially one with a history of addiction—is this: **how does he respond when you say no?**

Not just to a request. But to anything that limits his control, access, comfort, or entitlement.

Does he listen with humility? Or does he:

- Push past your "no"?
- Guilt-trip you for having boundaries?
- Frame your "no" as unforgiveness or rebellion?
- Sulk, explode, or punish you emotionally?

Because here's the truth: **real change respects limits. False repentance resents them.**

Saying "no" is one of the most powerful ways a woman can observe whether a man's transformation is genuine or performative. It's not just a boundary—it's a mirror. It reflects back the reality of what still lives inside him.

Anyone can say the right things for a while.

Anyone can cry.

Anyone can quote Scripture.

But only a man who is truly changing will honor your "no" without twisting it, resenting it, or retaliating against it.

That means:

- If you say, "I need space right now," and he pressures you? That's not repentance.
- If you say, "I'm not ready to reconcile," and he starts quoting verses about forgiveness? That's not repentance.
- If you say, "I need to protect the kids," and he accuses you of being bitter? That's not repentance.

Your "no" is not the problem.

Your "no" is a boundary God allows—even *commands*—you to have.

"Let what you say be simply 'Yes' or 'No'; anything more than this comes from evil." (Matthew 5:37, ESV)

Watch closely. Because how he handles your "no" will tell you more about his heart than any promise, plan, or prayer ever could.

An apology is not true unless it includes behavior change. Without that, apologies are meaningless. *You are not looking for an apology. You are looking for a truly transformed life.*

And that takes time. It takes consistency. It takes patience, external accountability, and a long track record. Without those things, reconciliation is not just unwise—it's unsafe.

The Cycle of Promises That Don't Last

One of the most disorienting experiences for women in abusive relationships is the repeated cycle of apologies, promises, and brief periods of seeming change—followed by a return to the same destructive behavior.

It's not just confusing. It's exhausting. And for women of faith, it's spiritually paralyzing. How many times do you forgive? How long do you wait? What if this time is really different?

Here's what often happens:

- He explodes, harms, or manipulates.
- He "breaks down" and apologizes.
- You're encouraged (or pressured) to forgive.
- He behaves for a while—sometimes days, some-times months.
- Then it happens again.

This pattern is not repentance. It's a behavioral cycle rooted in control. This is an example of intermittent reinforcement, which actually *strengthens* the trauma bond. The hope that this time he really means it keeps the victim emotionally tethered to him. The longer the cycle, the harder it becomes to break free.

This is why repeated promises without sustained behavioral change are dangerous. They mimic repentance just enough to make you doubt your own instincts—but they never produce lasting safety, peace, or mutual respect.

It's important to remember: **abuse is not a relationship problem. It's a character issue.** And character change doesn't happen because someone got caught or felt emotional. It happens when someone has a deep encounter with truth, repents fully, and begins a long-term journey of transformation.

Even then, trust must still be earned—not given just because someone is sorry.

You are allowed to say:

"I believe you're sorry. But I will wait to see if you are changed."

"Forgiveness does not mean reconciliation."

"I need a long, consistent track record of safety before I even consider restoration."

God does not ask you to risk your wellbeing for someone else's comfort. Reconciliation is only biblical when there has been true repentance. And true repentance doesn't fear being tested. It expects it.

In the next section, we'll address one of the most emotionally charged pieces of this journey: the pressure to reconcile—especially "for the kids."

The Pressure to Reconcile "For the Kids"

Few things weigh heavier on a mother's heart than her children. Many women remain in—or return to—abusive marriages because they believe it's the best way to protect their kids. Others are told by church leaders, counselors, or family members that reconciliation is "best for the children," especially if the father is now sober or claims to have changed.

But here's the truth: **children are not protected by a home that includes an abusive father. They are harmed by it—whether or not he's still using drugs or alcohol.**

An abusive man doesn't have to hit his children to hurt them. They absorb the fear in the home. They learn distorted patterns of love, power, gender, and responsibility. They often blame themselves for the chaos. Boys may become aggressive or emotionally shut down. Girls may grow up believing that control and dominance are normal in a relationship. And in some cases, the abuse eventually extends directly to the children themselves.

What message does it send to your kids if they see you crying, belittled, isolated, or broken—but continuing to stay?

Many Christian mothers are told that staying in the home gives them a chance to "influence the family spiritually." But staying in a spiritually abusive marriage is not a godly witness—it's a dangerous burden that God never intended you to carry alone.

You are not failing your children by leaving an abuser. You are protecting them. You are showing them what boundaries look like. You are modeling courage, dignity, and trust in a God who sees and saves. Even if they're too young to understand it now, one day they will know: *"My mom refused to let evil stay hidden. She chose safety and truth."*

If your church, counselor, or family tells you that your only faithful option is to go back—for the kids—you have every right to push back with the truth: you are being faithful by protecting what God loves.

And He loves you. He loves your children. He is not honored by a home that uses His name to cover up destruction.

In the next section, we'll talk about what real, lasting change looks like over time—and why you are not obligated to believe in it without evidence.

The Role of Time and Fruit

Real change takes time—and it shows up as fruit, not just feelings.

In Luke 6:44, Jesus said, *"Each tree is recognized by its own fruit."* A man may say all the right things. He may pray, cry, quote Scripture, and claim he's different. But the question isn't what he says—it's what he produces. Has he changed the way he treats you and your children? Has he stopped demanding, blaming, and controlling? Has he taken responsibility without being forced?

Too often, women are pushed to reconcile based on words or temporary behavior—when what's really needed is a consistent track record over a long period of time.

Here's what fruit looks like:

- He respects boundaries without resentment.
- He no longer tries to control, intimidate, or manipulate.
- He accepts a separation or divorce without demanding restoration.
- He supports his children out of responsibility, not as leverage.
- He places himself under real, outside accountability (not just his pastor or friends).
- He acknowledges the full impact of his actions—and makes no excuses.

Time reveals truth. And truth can be seen in the consistency (or lack thereof) of the fruit of the Spirit as listed in Galatians 5:22-23: *But the fruit of the Spirit is love, joy, peace, patience, kindness, goodness, faithfulness, gentleness, self-control; against such things there is no law.*"

You are not unloving, unforgiving, or faithless for waiting to see fruit. In fact, Scripture commends discernment. Proverbs 14:15 says, *"The simple believe anything, but the prudent give thought to their steps."*

You are allowed to say:

- *"I forgive you, but I don't trust you."*
- *"I wish you well, but I cannot be in a relationship with you."*

- "I will observe your actions over time. If there is lasting change, then we can talk."

Forgiveness is a gift you offer to God. **Trust must be earned.**

Reconciliation is not automatic. It is the fruit of true repentance—demonstrated in humility, time, and hard-won transformation. **And sometimes, the damage done throughout the years is too much for restoration of the marriage to ever take place.** Reconciliation may look like co-parenting with peace and support for each other and the children without being married again or continuing the marriage.

What He Needs Most from You

There's a saying: **people don't change until the pain of staying the same becomes greater than the pain of change.** Think about that. The pain that prompts real transformation might be circumstantial, medical, or relational. But as long as staying the same feels comfortable, there's no reason to change—until it isn't anymore.

So, what if the most loving thing you can do is say "no"? What if love sometimes looks like creating distance, drawing a line, and saying, "This far, and no farther"?

I cringe when I hear a man's testimony celebrating his "long-suffering" wife who stayed for forty years while he repeatedly ran rampant over her heart. What if she had said "no more" sooner? What if her refusal to tolerate the abuse had been the very thing that could have opened the door to real change?

Let's be clear: setting strong boundaries does *not* guarantee that he will change. And that's not why you do it. Boundaries are not weapons or ultimatums. They are not meant to manipulate him into better behavior. True and lasting transformation must come from within—not from fear, shame, or the pressure to perform. A man who only puts on a mask of change to get you back has not changed at all.

But when you draw a firm line—when you remove yourself and your children from the path of destruction—you at least give him the opportunity to face the truth. You stop participating in the dance. And that may be the first time he's ever had to confront what his actions have truly cost.

Statistically, most abusers do not change. These are hard words, but necessary ones. For a man to genuinely repent of how he has sinned against you—not just in addiction, but in the patterns of control, cruelty, and coercion—the cycle must be broken. And you are the only one who can break it.

You are not responsible for his choices.

But you are responsible for protecting your life, your children, and your sanity.

You are not unloving for saying "enough."

You are being faithful to the truth.

There are resources available for men who want help changing from an abuser to a safe person. Some suggestions would be the following:

G5 ministry (for men). G5men@calledtopeace.org. This is part of the Called To Peace Ministries organization. This is a description of their program:

The G5 Men's Abuse Intervention Course

G5 is an educational support and accountability course for men who have been destructive in relationships. The G5 Men's Course is an abuse intervention course for men who have used coercive and controlling tactics in their intimate relationships. Men have been referred to G5 through various sources, although the program does not participate with men who are court ordered. Wives are also encouraged to request an advocate through Called To Peace Ministries (CTPM) also.

Domestic abuse is primarily a male man-problem that impacts women and children at an alarming rate. Our aim is to help husbands, boyfriends, and fathers recognize the patterns of hurtful and destructive behavior present in their relationships. G5 is a 26 week virtual educational accountability course. Every participant that willingly submits to the process will build a local accountability team to further encourage, challenge, and hold them accountable to the changes they say they intend to make for peace, healing, and trust to be established in their relationships. They will do the weekly homework calling them to intentionally reflect on their past and recent behavior noting the impacts thereof on their spouse, children, and relationship with God. Participants then use information gleaned from these assignments to develop their own Personal Change Plan. The Personal Change plan will be the G5-Man's and his A-Team's marching orders going forward and beyond the G5 Course. The participants that are serious about changing for the better will review and update their plans regularly.

The best way to gain information about the G5 Men's Course is to email: G5men@calledtopeace.org.

PeaceWorks University – Chris Moles, ChrisMoles. org. – Men of Peace Self-Paced Course. According to the website, "The Men of Peace Self-Paced Course is the compilation of all of Chris Mole's past Men of Peace coaching content plus brand-new material. This course will walk men through the three-fold Men of Peace process of Information, Transformation, and Reformation."

In the final section, we'll return to where we began: your heart, your safety, and God's care for you—not just as a wife or mother, but as His beloved daughter.

Final Reflection: God Sees the Heart

You may still wrestle with doubt. *What if I'm being too harsh? What if he really is trying? What if God wants me to reconcile?* These questions can feel like spiritual quicksand—especially when others are telling you to soften, forgive, or go back.

But here's what you need to know: **God sees the heart.** Not just his—but yours.

He sees your weariness.

He sees the tears no one else saw.

He sees the nights you begged Him for help, and the strength it took to walk away when everything in your world said you shouldn't.

And He sees your love for truth, even when it costs you everything.

You are not rebellious for requiring repentance. You are not faithless for needing time. You are not unforgiving for protecting your body, your heart, or your children.

God never asked you to be a martyr to someone else's sin. He does not call staying in harm's way an act of love. He calls love *patient, kind, not boastful, not proud, not rude, not self-seeking, not easily angered, and keeping no record of wrongs* (1 Corinthians 13). That love must go both ways. If it doesn't, it isn't love—it's bondage dressed in religious language.

You may still feel unsure about what to do next. That's okay. Clarity comes in time. Your job is not to force an answer but to walk in truth one step at a time.

If he has truly changed, the fruit will speak for itself.

And if he hasn't, that isn't your failure—it's his.

You are still responsible to walk in the light. To protect what God has entrusted to you. To heal. To live free. To remember that reconciliation with an unrepentant abuser is not a holy requirement—it is a trap.

God honors truth. He honors wisdom. And He honors you.

Chapter 12 Discussion Questions

1. **Hope or "Hopium"?**

    When you picture your partner finally changing, what specific behaviors do you imagine will be different? Which of those have you actually seen—consistently and without pressure—from him so far?

2. **Charm vs. Change**

    Think back to a recent apology or "repentant" moment. Which parts felt like true humility, and which parts felt like image-management or emotional manipulation?

3. **Testing the Fruit**

    Galatians 5:22-23 lists the fruit of the Spirit. Which fruit is still missing behind closed doors? How long will you require consistent evidence before you consider trust or reconciliation?

4. **Your "No" as a Mirror**

    Recall the last time you said "no" to something he wanted (sex, money, access, reconciliation). How did he respond? What does that reaction reveal about whether control or change is driving him?

5. **Accountability or Appearance?**

Is your partner pursuing outside accountability that **you** can verify (licensed counselor, certified batterer-intervention program, trauma-informed pastor), or is he hand-picking allies who will vouch for him? How transparent is the process?

6. **Consequences Without Complaints**

True repentance accepts consequences. Has he shown willingness to honor boundaries such as financial transparency, protective orders, supervised visitation, or a prolonged separation—even when it's uncomfortable for him?

7. **Pressure Points**

Who is urging you to reconcile quickly—church leaders, family, friends, even your partner? How does that pressure affect your discernment? What would it look like to give yourself unhurried time and space?

8. **Protecting the Children**

How does his behavior—sober but still controlling or volatile—impact your children's sense of safety? What would godly stewardship of their well-being require right now?

9. **"Seven Times Leave" Statistic**

Abused women leave an average of seven times before leaving for good. Where do you see yourself in that cycle? What would have to change, concretely and consistently, for you not to repeat past returns?

10. **Godly Sorrow or Worldly Sorrow**

    Read 2 Corinthians 7:10-11. Which evidences of **godly sorrow** (earnestness, eagerness for justice, alarm at harm done) have you witnessed? Which signs of **worldly sorrow** (tears but no change, regret over consequences, self-pity) keep resurfacing?

Use these questions privately or with a trusted, trauma-informed counselor or support group. Let them guide you toward clarity rooted in truth—not in pressure, fear, or wishful thinking.

Chapter 13:

THE WOMAN'S JOURNEY— BREAKING FREE FROM ABUSE

"When someone has showed you over a period of time that they don't have your best interests at heart, why allow them to be the loudest voice in your life?"

— Lysa TerKeurst

Ashley's Story

I came to Christ when I was thirteen, quietly and on my own. My family went to church, but what happened inside our home was anything but Christian. Abuse—emotional, verbal, and sexual—was part of the atmosphere. When I gave my life to Jesus, I sensed the Holy Spirit telling me not to share it with them. It would be like casting pearls before swine.

We weren't allowed to use the phone or dress in modern styles. I was mocked both at school and at church. I never dated and didn't want friends to come over—my parents were too controlling and critical. I excelled in school and was even invited to skip my senior year for my achievements in art, but my father, an educator himself, said women didn't need an education. I started community college with no help or encouragement.

That's when I met him.

He approached me after church and asked for a ride home. He shared a powerful testimony—how God had saved him from drug addiction. He said he was planning to attend Bible college, and his entire family had come to Christ. His passion seemed real, his family warm and welcoming. They were loud, affectionate, and different from everything I'd known. It felt like hope.

We began writing letters while he was away at school. When he came home for a break, we spent time together. He was my first boyfriend, my first kiss. There was no sex at that point, and he seemed respectful. But when my parents found out, they gave me an ultimatum: leave him or lose everything. In front of my siblings, they said I could either end the relationship or give up my home, my car, and my schooling. I wasn't even asked how I felt.

I left.

Some church friends helped me at first, and then his family offered me a place to stay. That's when the shift began. He started controlling little things—like a silver coin my grandfather gave me. He claimed I was idolizing it and pressured me until I finally dropped it in the church offering plate just to make the harassment stop.

Soon, I was pregnant. He insisted we were married "in God's eyes" and pushed for a small civil wedding. We moved into a small place near his family. I hoped we'd build a life together. Instead, the abuse escalated.

He hit me for not having dinner ready. He criticized everything—my cooking, my housekeeping, my parenting. He forced sex on me—often at night, while I was exhausted or asleep. He didn't care if I said no. I became pregnant again and again. He sabotaged my birth control and used Scripture to guilt and control me. He turned our home into a prison and called it headship.

I started working again and slowly began to find my voice. I began pushing back, refusing to be silent. That's when he turned his anger on our children—especially our oldest son. I tried to protect them, but I felt trapped and overwhelmed.

A pastor's wife finally spoke what I couldn't say out loud: "This is not God's will for your life. Staying in this is not a testimony to Christ." Her words cracked something open in me. I began to see clearly for the first time.

I applied for nursing school while working nights as a waitress. Every step of the way, he resisted. He stalked me, violated restraining orders, emptied our bank account, and manipulated the children—especially our oldest. But I kept going.

I made it through nursing school—barely—fighting exhaustion, fear, and deep spiritual confusion. God provided everything I needed: financial aid, safe housing, scholarships, and a Christian support group that opened my eyes. Through them, I realized I had made my abuser an idol. I had been serving him, not Christ.

But no more.

I graduated, got my first paycheck as an RN, and took my kids out for Chinese food. It may not sound like much, but it was a celebration. I had survived. The abuse hadn't ended all at once, and the scars still ran deep—but the story didn't end in the dark.

There is life on the other side.

Now, I want other women to know: if this is your story, you are not alone. You are not crazy. God is not asking you to suffer in silence or stay under abuse. There is a way out—and God will be with you every step of the way."

Ashley's story is just one of many. And while each woman's path looks different, the ache underneath is often the same—confusion, fear, isolation, and a quiet but persistent longing to be free.

But breaking free from abuse isn't just about leaving a person or a place. It's about untangling the lies that have taken root inside us. Lies about who we are. About what love is. About what God expects from us.

For many women, the moment they physically leave is only the beginning. What follows is a longer, more hidden journey—healing from guilt, shame, and over-responsibility. Relearning how to trust yourself, how to hear God clearly, and how to protect what matters.

And for those with children, that journey becomes even more layered. Custody battles, fear of retaliation, courts that don't always see clearly—these are burdens no mother should have to bear alone. The tension between protecting your children and trying to survive yourself can feel suffocating. But there is help. There is wisdom. And you are not crazy for caring this deeply.

It is here, in the tender and often painful work of reclaiming your voice and your value, that the real freedom begins.

Guilt and Shame

If fear is the chain that holds many women in abusive relationships, guilt and shame are the locks that keep the chain fastened.

Abuse thrives in the fog of confusion—but especially in the confusion between false guilt and true conviction. True conviction, prompted by the Holy Spirit, leads us to repentance and healing. False guilt, on the other hand, is a weapon of the enemy. It keeps us stuck in cycles of self-blame for things we did not cause and cannot control.

We often hear the words guilt and shame used interchangeably, but they are not the same. Guilt says that I have done something wrong. Shame says that I was made wrong, that I am completely flawed. I may say "I feel guilty for..." some infraction, such as losing my temper or whatever. Shame is an underlying current that runs through our lives ever since our ancestors Adam and Eve chose to disobey God—shame entered the world at that moment, along with sin. Adam and Eve hid from God and tried to sew leaves together to hide their nakedness. No one told them to do that. It became part of their core being (and ours) from that moment on.

> *"Shame is a focus on self, guilt is a focus on behavior. Shame is 'I am bad.' Guilt is 'I did something bad.'"*
> — Brené Brown, Daring Greatly

"Shame corrodes the very part of us that believes we are capable of change."

— Brené Brown, I Thought
It Was Just Me (But It Isn't)

Abusers often use guilt as a tool of control. Spiritual abuse adds even more weight:

"God hates divorce."
"You're failing as a wife and a Christian."

Over time, this emotional and spiritual manipulation causes women to internalize a deep, toxic shame. But shame was never meant to be your inheritance.

"Those who look to Him are radiant, and their faces are never covered in shame." (Psalm 34:5)

When you feel shame over walking away from abuse, remember: it is not your sin you are fleeing—it is his.

"Therefore, there is now no condemnation for those who are in Christ Jesus." (Romans 8:1)

The voice of shame is not the voice of your Shepherd. Listen instead to the One who calls you daughter.

Over-functioning: Doing All the Work

You've likely been doing it all. Managing the emotions, the parenting, the spiritual temperature, the recovery process. Carrying the weight of two people for far too long. This is not love. It's over-functioning—a survival mechanism dressed up as virtue.

> "Come to Me, all who are weary and burdened, and I will give you rest." (Matthew 11:28)

You were never meant to carry what only God can redeem. When you stop over-functioning, the illusion may collapse. That's okay. Let it fall. Because what remains will be real—and the beginning of something true.

You are allowed to stop.

You are allowed to rest.

You are allowed to be free.

The Dangers of Marriage Counseling in Abusive Situations

For many women in faith-based communities, marriage counseling is presented as the go-to solution for a struggling relationship. Pastors recommend it. Friends suggest it. Sometimes, it's a requirement before church leaders will even *consider* supporting a separation.

But here's the truth too many survivors learn the hard way:

Marriage counseling is not safe—or effective—in abusive relationships.

Marriage counseling assumes a basic level of mutual goodwill, emotional safety, and shared responsibility. It is designed for couples who both want the relationship to heal and are willing to own their part in the breakdown.

Abuse does not work like that.

In abusive dynamics—especially where addiction has played a role—there is a fundamental imbalance of power and control. And when that imbalance is brought into the counseling room, it often gets spiritualized, minimized, or ignored.

How Abusers Use Counseling as a Weapon

In many cases, abusers use marriage counseling not as a tool for change but as a stage to perform.

1. They charm the counselor, then rage at home.
2. They paint themselves as victims of their wife's unforgiveness.
3. They admit to just enough wrongdoing to look "humble," but never enough to take real accountability.
4. They use the counselor's language to manipulate her later: *"Even our counselor said you need to work on your tone."*

Some women have said they felt more unsafe in because of counseling than they did at home previously, because now their abuser had new tools, new language, and new ways to twist Scripture and therapy against them. Anything she said in counseling could and would be used against her in the future. It became a tool in the abuser's arsenal of things to throw in her face.

When Counseling Makes It Worse

What happens when a counselor, unaware of the abuse, tells the woman to work harder on communication? To try to understand his triggers? To pray for unity and stop "withholding love"?

It reinforces the very messages she's been trying to unlearn.

It deepens the trauma.

And in some cases, it makes it nearly impossible for her to leave—because now even the professionals are siding with her abuser. Counselors are human and can be swayed by someone's glib talk or seemingly sincere desires to change and be a good partner/father. But the counselor is not there when the mask comes off and the weapons come out.

What the Survivors Needed Instead

What these women needed was not couples therapy. They needed safety. Truth-telling. Clarity.

They needed a counselor who understood abuse dynamics, trauma bonding, and the cycle of manipulation. They needed someone who would look them in the eye and say: "You're not crazy. This is not normal. And you are allowed to want safety."

Safe Alternatives

In abusive situations, individual counseling with a trauma-informed therapist is often the best first step—**for the survivor alone**. Not to fix the marriage. Not to figure out how to "be better." But to reclaim her mind, her sanity, her voice.

If the abuser wants help, he must pursue it separately and over time—with a focus on repentance and accountability, not reconciliation.

Some churches and ministries now offer separation counseling or accountability-based interventions where safety, not restoration, is the goal. But these are rare. Most survivors must discern that **not all counseling is safe counseling**.

A Word for the Church

If you're a pastor, elder, or ministry leader reading this: **Please stop sending abused women into marriage counseling with their abusers.** Abuse is not a marriage problem. It is an abuse problem. Mariage counseling doesn't save marriages in this case. It reinforces bondage. Abusers consistently take what is said in marriage counseling and use it against their spouse.

Jesus never once told a woman to return to the person harming her. He stood between her and her accusers. He offered truth, dignity, and freedom.

If we are to represent Him well, we must do the same.

Rebuilding Trust: What Can and Can't Be Restored

Abuse doesn't just destroy safety. It erodes something even deeper: trust.

Not just trust in him.

But trust in *yourself.*

Trust in what's true.

And often, tragically—trust in God.

You second-guess your instincts. You doubt your own memories. You are wary of other people. You question your discernment. And if the abuse was spiritual in nature, it can feel like your very relationship with God has been used against you.

Before trust can be rebuilt with anyone else, it must begin here: **within you.**

Trusting Yourself Again

One of the most devastating effects of coercive control is how it rewires a woman's sense of self. Gaslighting, blame-shifting, spiritual manipulation—they all teach her to override her intuition.

"Maybe I'm the problem."

"Maybe I'm overreacting."

"Maybe I misunderstood what God was saying."

Rebuilding trust means relearning how to listen to that still, small voice within you. The voice that sensed something was wrong long before you had the words. The voice the Holy Spirit *never stopped whispering*—even when others tried to drown it out.

You may not trust everything right now. That's okay. But you can start with this: **You are not crazy. And you can trust your process of healing.**

Trusting God Again

Many women in faith-based abuse feel betrayed—not just by their husbands or their churches, but by God Himself.

"Why didn't You protect me?"

"Why did You allow this?"

"Why didn't You open the eyes of the people I cried out to?"

These questions are not signs of rebellion. They are signs of a heart that is faithful—and devastated. They are the cries of someone who loved deeply, obeyed sincerely, and was wounded in the very place she thought would be safe.

Rebuilding trust in God does not mean pretending those questions don't exist. It means daring to bring them to Him—raw, trembling, honest. It means rediscovering the God who sees (El Roi), the God who rescues the oppressed, the God who never once condoned what was done in His name.

Healing begins when we stop confusing the character of Christ with the actions of those who abused His authority.

What About Trusting My Husband Again?

This is the question many women dread:

"Should I ever trust him again?"

The short answer? **Not unless he earns it—and not just once, but over time and with consistency.**

Trust is not owed.

Forgiveness does not require reconciliation.

And biblical love does not mean setting yourself up to be hurt again.

True repentance looks like humility, accountability, long-term change, and a willingness to accept the consequences of past harm. It is not a single tearful apology. It is not a few good weeks. It is time and consistency—a track record of safety, truth, and respect. If that is not present, trust should not be either.

Too many women have been told, "*You need to trust again, or your marriage will never heal.*" But that puts the burden back on her shoulders—when the real burden of restoration belongs to the one who broke it.

You are not hard-hearted for being cautious.

You are not unforgiving for guarding your heart.

You are wise. You are discerning. You are healing.

And **real trust can only grow in the soil of truth—watered by time and consistency.**

Finances, Housing, and Legal Issues (With or Without Children)

For many women, the decision to leave an abusive relationship isn't stopped by love or loyalty—it's stopped by money.

He controls the bank account.

She doesn't have access to passwords or credit cards.

She may not have worked in years—or ever.

She's afraid that if she leaves, she'll end up homeless... or in court.

And if children are involved, the stakes feel even higher.

This is not weakness. This is years of **coercive control**. And it's not uncommon. Financial abuse is one of the most effective tools an abuser uses to keep his partner trapped—because it isolates, disempowers, and creates deep dependency.

Financial Abuse: What It Looks Like

He monitors her spending, even on necessities.

She has no access to bank accounts or joint assets.

He sabotages her ability to work or build a career.

He racks up debt in her name.

He forces her to justify every dollar or beg for money.

Financial abuse leaves lasting scars—not just in the bank account, but in a woman's sense of confidence and security. Many women stay, not because they don't want freedom, but because they see no viable path out.

Planning for Stability

If you're reading this and feeling stuck, you're not alone—and there *is* help.

Here are some foundational steps many women take to prepare for stability:

1. Gather documents: Birth certificates, marriage licenses, passports, insurance papers, pay stubs, bank records. Make copies and store them safely outside the home if needed.

2. Open a private bank account in your name only, at a different bank.

3. Begin saving cash quietly: Even small amounts add up. Hide it in safe places or with a trusted person.

4. Find legal advice early: Many areas have free or sliding-scale legal clinics for women, including Christian organizations with a trauma-informed perspective.

5. Research shelters and transitional housing: Especially those that understand domestic violence and spiritual abuse dynamics.

With Children: Custody and Child Support

If you have children, everything becomes more complex—and more urgent.

- Family courts often prioritize shared parenting, even when abuse is present. This can be deeply disheartening, but documenting the abuse clearly and consistently is critical.
- Keep records: Text messages, emails, incident logs, medical visits, school reports—anything that demonstrates patterns of control, neglect, or harm.
- Consider parallel parenting over co-parenting: this limits contact with the abuser and creates more structure.

- Seek support: There are advocacy groups that specialize in helping protective mothers navigate custody battles. Called to Peace is one such group that is doing excellent advocacy work.

Without Children: The Fear of Starting Over Alone

Women without children may hear things like: **"At least you don't have to worry about custody."** But that doesn't mean the pain or risk is any less. In some ways, it's even harder to justify leaving when "only" your own safety is at stake—especially in Christian circles where motherhood is often seen as the highest justification for making hard choices.

When there are no children to protect, many women struggle to believe that protecting *themselves* is a valid reason to leave. The lie creeps in:

"Maybe it's not that bad."
"Maybe I should stay and keep trying."
"Maybe I'm being selfish."

But your safety still matters.

Your life still matters.

You are not selfish for wanting to survive.

And then there's the loneliness.

For many women, especially in faith communities, leaving an abusive relationship also means leaving a social structure.

You're no longer part of a couple. You may lose friendships that were once "ours." You may feel like the third wheel, or find yourself excluded from the gatherings you once belonged to.

There's often a quiet grief in realizing that people you loved and trusted don't know how—or choose not—to walk with you through this.

You may fear sitting alone in church. You may fear being the only one at the table without a plus-one. You may fear never being loved again.

These fears are real. And they are painful. But they are not permanent.

Mia's Story

Mia didn't have kids, which meant people often assumed things were easier for her.

"At least you don't have to worry about custody," they said.

"At least you can just walk away."

But walking away didn't feel easy. Not at all.

She and her husband had been married for eight years. They met at a Christian conference after her husband had gone through rehab, served in church together, and led a couples' small group. From the outside, they looked like the perfect pair. But behind closed doors, things were different.

He never hit her. But he used words like weapons—sharpened with sarcasm, cold silence, spiritual guilt, and subtle control. He monitored her spending, made cruel jokes about her weight, and regularly reminded her that no one else would ever love her like he did. She stopped sharing with friends because they wouldn't understand. And deep down, she wasn't sure she did either.

Over time, she began to shrink—emotionally, spiritually, even physically. She felt like a ghost in her own home.

When she finally confided in a friend from church, the response was well-meaning but dismissive. "Maybe you're just going through a rough patch," the friend said. "Have you prayed about your attitude?"

Mia felt the walls closing in.

The fear wasn't just about leaving him—it was about losing everything else. The couple friends. The Bible study. The social calendar. The shared friendships that would inevitably choose him over her. She imagined showing up at church alone and being met with silence—or worse, pity.

And yet... she couldn't deny the quiet voice that had started to rise up within her.

"You were not made for this."

"You are allowed to leave."

"You are worth protecting."

She didn't leave all at once. She started by journaling the truth. She quietly opened a separate bank account. She found a counselor who understood spiritual abuse. And one day, she walked out—not because it was easy, but because it was right.

Now, years later, Mia says the hardest part wasn't walking away from him. It was walking away from the illusion that staying made her more faithful. It was grieving the friendships that disappeared and the community that stayed silent.

But what she found on the other side was better than what she left behind. She found her voice again. She found new friendships. She found rest.

She found herself.

Facing the Fear of Violence and Retaliation

For some women, the question isn't just *Should I leave?* It's *Will I survive if I do?*

The fear of retaliation is very real. Abusive men—especially those with a history of addiction, control, or rage—often do not take rejection quietly. And far too many women have heard threats like:

"If you leave me, I'll make sure you regret it."
"You'll never see the kids again."
"I'll ruin you."
"If I can't have you, no one will."

These aren't empty words. They're warnings. And ignoring them can be dangerous.

Leaving an abuser is **one of the most dangerous times in a woman's life.** Studies show that the risk of lethal violence escalates significantly in the weeks and months after a woman leaves.

That does not mean you're doomed.

It means you need a plan.

You Are Not Overreacting

Fear of violence is often downplayed by others:

- *"You're being dramatic."*
- *"He wouldn't really hurt you."*
- *"He's just saying that out of anger."*

But let's be honest—you know him. You've seen what he's capable of. And even if you haven't been physically assaulted, many abusive men escalate only after they lose control of the woman. That's when threats become action. When words become weapons. When emotional abuse turns physical.

Your fear is not a lack of faith. It's wisdom.

Safety Planning: You Don't Have to Do This Alone

Creating a safety plan can be the difference between chaos and clarity. A good plan includes:

- A safe person or place you can go at a moment's notice.
- Packed essentials stored discreetly (ID, cash, meds, keys) stashed in a "go bag."
- A scripted excuse if you need to leave quickly.
- Turning off location sharing or smart tracking from shared devices.
- Alerting trusted allies who can check on you regularly.

- Notifying your child's school and providing legal documents if needed.
- Working with a domestic violence advocate to walk you through your options.

You are not being paranoid. You are being prepared.

It is important to avoid telling your abuser the exact date or details of your departure or even that you are planning to leave. Work with advocates, shelters, and legal professionals to stay one step ahead. This may feel dishonest, but it is essential for your safety.

Emergency Go-Bag Checklist

Essentials to pack in case you need to leave quickly

> "The prudent see danger and take refuge, but the simple keep going and pay the penalty.'
> — Proverbs 27:12

Identification & Important Documents

- Driver's license or photo ID
- Social Security cards (yours and your children's)
- Birth certificates (yours and your children's)
- Passports

- Health insurance cards
- Marriage/divorce papers
- Custody or protection orders
- Any legal or immigration paperwork
- Recent photos of your children (in case of abduction risk)

Money & Financial Essentials

- Cash (even small amounts are useful)
- Prepaid debit card (if you can get one)
- Credit card (if in your name only)
- Checkbook (if applicable)
- Copy of bank account info (hidden or disguised)

Phone & Communication

- Fully charged backup phone (if possible)
- Phone charger and/or power bank
- List of emergency contacts (written down in case you lose access to your phone)

Clothing & Personal Items

- A few changes of clothes for you and your children
- Comfortable shoes

- Jacket or hoodie
- Undergarments and socks
- Small bag with toiletries:

  o Toothbrush and toothpaste
  o Deodorant
  o Soap
  o Feminine hygiene items
  o Hairbrush or comb
  o Prescriptions and essential medications (in original bottles if possible)

Faith & Encouragement

- Small Bible or devotional
- Journal and pen
- List of affirming Scriptures or truths
- Letter to yourself reminding you why you're leaving

If You Have Children

- Diapers, wipes, and formula if needed
- Snack pouches, juice boxes, sippy cups
- Extra clothes and shoes
- Favorite small toy, book, or stuffed animal
- Medication or allergy supplies

- School records or special needs documentation (if applicable)

Other Helpful Items

- Spare keys: car, house, or storage
- Flash drive with important digital records
- Recent utility bills (to help prove residency later)
- Safety plan (written with advocate, if applicable)
- List of safe shelters, hotlines, or people who can help

Where to Keep Your Go-Bag

- At a trusted friend's house, your workplace, or in your car trunk (if safe)
- Hidden in your home in a place your abuser is unlikely to check
- Broken up into smaller bags if necessary (disguise some as gym bags, diaper bags, etc.)

A Note on Secrecy & Safety

I cannot emphasize this enough: do not tell your abuser about your plan. Do not leave the bag in a visible place. Use caution and discernment. A domestic violence advocate can help you customize your plan based on your situation.

Custody Battles and Co-Parenting When Addiction or Abuse Still Lurks Beneath the Surface

Caitlyn's Story

She had no bruises. No restraining order. No police report.

But what she did have was a growing sense of dread every time she had to send her children to their father's house.

Everyone around her said she should be grateful—he was clean now. Holding down a job. Attending church again. Even quoting Bible verses about reconciliation.

But she saw the cracks. The late-night calls where his words slurred just enough. The shiftiness in his eyes when she asked simple questions. The way their son came home withdrawn, or hyper, or unsettled, but couldn't—or wouldn't—say why.

She told her attorney she was worried.

She told the court that something felt off.

She even tried to explain how his past porn use had shaped their home, how he pressured their daughter about modesty in ways that felt... wrong.

But she had no proof. And the judge didn't see what she saw.

Now she waits by the phone during every weekend visit. She prays over her kids every time they leave. She documents everything. And she lives in the tension of being called "bitter" for trying to protect her children from a man the court says is safe—but her spirit says otherwise.

When He's Clean on Paper, But Not Safe in Reality

Abusive men can be very convincing in court. If he's sober now, gainfully employed, and "in recovery," he may present himself as the reformed father just trying to reconnect with his children. Meanwhile:

- He uses visitation as a way to manipulate or punish you.
- He exposes your kids to harmful people or unsafe environments.
- He subtly turns them against you with charm and guilt.
- He pressures them to keep secrets.
- He talks about you in spiritualized or demeaning terms.

All while appearing squeaky clean to the judge. And if you raise concerns—especially about pornography, emotional abuse, or suspected substance use without evidence—you risk being labeled bitter, controlling, or uncooperative. This is why so many women feel terrified and silenced by the very system meant to protect them.

Porn Use and the Courts: The Invisible Threat

In Christian homes, many women rightly recognize that ongoing porn use is a form of sexual infidelity and spiritual harm. But in most court systems, porn addiction is not recognized as abuse. In fact, raising it as a concern can backfire, making you look rigid, religiously extreme, or emotionally unstable.

But let's be clear:

- Porn use *does* affect children, even if they aren't shown it directly.
- It *does* shape the emotional and spiritual environment of a home.
- And when combined with past addiction or abuse, it is often a sign that deeper harm is still present.

Even if the court won't name it, you can.

How to Navigate the System Without Losing Yourself

You may not be able to control the court's decision. But you can:

1. Document everything: Keep logs of behaviors, changes in your children, concerning comments. Don't assume the truth will "speak for itself."

2. Avoid reactive language: Use facts, not feelings. Say "He dropped them off an hour late and smelled of alcohol" rather than "He's falling apart again."

3. Build your credibility: Show consistency, calmness, and a commitment to the children's well-being—not retaliation.

4. Use the term 'parallel parenting': Not co-parenting. You don't need to "work together" with someone who is unrepentant. You need legal clarity and strong boundaries.

5. Pray and prepare: Ask God to reveal hidden things in His timing. But don't delay safety decisions waiting for others to believe what you already know. Sarah McDugal at Wilderness to Wild and Called to Peace Ministries have excellent resources for navigating this very tough issue.

When Your Kids Are Involved and You're Not Believed

This is one of the most painful places to be. You see the risk. You live with the dread. But no one listens.

This does not make you a bad mother.

It makes you a brave one.

Your children may not understand your choices now. But one day, they will look back—and they will see a mother who stood between them and danger, even when the world told her to sit down.

"Speak up for those who cannot speak for themselves; ensure justice for those being crushed."

(Proverbs 31:8, NLT)

God sees. God knows. And your advocacy is not wasted.

Reflection

You've walked through some of the hardest terrain a woman can face—guilt, spiritual confusion, broken trust, legal intimidation, and deep emotional loss. And still, you are standing.

Maybe not steadily. Maybe not with certainty. But you are still here. That matters.

In the aftermath of abuse—especially when it's entangled with addiction, faith, or family—one of the most radical, redemptive things a woman can do is begin to reclaim her boundaries. Not to punish. Not to harden. But to protect what God is restoring.

It's time to explore what it means to guard your heart *without* shutting it down. To set limits *without* shame. To live as someone whose life, body, and soul truly matter—because they do.

In the next chapter, we will talk further about boundaries: what they are and what they aren't. Learning to have healthy boundaries is often one of the biggest hurdles to cross in our healing process.

Chapter 13 Discussion Questions

1. **Ashley's Story**
- What parts of Ashley's story resonated with your own experience? What emotions did it stir?
- Have you ever felt silenced by people who should have protected you? What would you say now if you had your voice back?

2. **Guilt and Shame**
- How have guilt or shame been used to keep you in harmful situations?
- Can you identify a moment when you confused false guilt for true conviction? What helped you see the difference?

3. **Over-Functioning**
- In what ways have you taken on too much responsibility in your relationship or home?
- What would it look like to let go of something God never asked you to carry?

4. The Dangers of Marriage Counseling in Abusive Situations

- Have you ever been pressured into counseling that made things worse? What would a *safe* counseling experience look like for you?
- How can you begin to trust your discernment again after being spiritually or professionally gaslit?

5. Rebuilding Trust

- What do you most struggle to trust right now—yourself, God, or others? Why?
- What would rebuilding trust with yourself look like in this season?

6. Finances, Housing, and Legal Fears

- What are your greatest fears about leaving—or staying— in an abusive relationship when it comes to money or legal protection?
- What step can you take today, however small, to move toward stability or preparation?

7. Facing the Fear of Retaliation

- What has your body or intuition told you about your safety? Have you been ignoring those signals?
- Who can help you build a safety plan—even in secret—if you need it?

8. **Custody Battles and Being Disbelieved**
- If you've been disbelieved by the courts, church, or family, how has that affected you emotionally or spiritually?
- What truths about your children's needs do you want to keep holding onto, even when no one else sees them?

9. **What safety planning can you do now, whether or not you plan to leave the marriage?**

10. **Final Reflection**
- What would it mean to believe that your safety, dignity, and freedom matter just as much to God as your children's?
- What do you need to hear from Jesus today as you walk this journey?

Chapter 14:

BOUNDARIES ARE THE MOST LOVING THING YOU CAN DO

Setting Healthy, Biblical Boundaries

Boundaries are not selfish—they are biblical.

Jesus set boundaries. Paul set boundaries. Scripture calls us to wisdom and self-control, not constant exposure to harm. But many women—especially those shaped by addiction, trauma, or spiritual distortion—were taught a false gospel: that passivity is holiness, and love means being endlessly available to pain, no matter the cost.

Setting a boundary doesn't make you unloving. It means you're no longer participating in a lie. It says, *"I am made in the image of God. I love you, but I will not allow your sin to dominate my life."*

Boundaries clarify what is healthy, safe, and true. And even when external boundaries can't yet be drawn—because of circumstance, finances, or fear—internal boundaries can begin. You can start saying *no* in your heart, mind, and spirit long before you say it out loud. And that is holy.

A Tale of Two Houses

When I was a young girl, I often rode horses through the fire roads behind our property. We could ride for hours without seeing a single house. One day, though, we discovered an old hunting cabin deep in the woods. It had no glass in the windows, no lock on the doors, and clearly no protection. Anyone could walk in. There was nothing to keep them out.

That cabin reminds me of what it's like to live without boundaries—open to anything and everyone. It may look adventurous or generous, but in reality, it's vulnerable to trespassers and destruction.

Now contrast that with the White House. The entire perimeter is guarded by a tall, well-monitored fence. It doesn't mean the President is imprisoned. The fence isn't to keep people in—it's to keep danger out. No one jumps that fence without consequences.

In the same way, boundaries aren't about shutting out love or freedom. They are about protecting what's valuable—what God is building in your life. **Your heart is not an abandoned cabin. It is a holy home.**

Boundaries and Your True Identity Who You Are in Christ

We must start here. Boundaries are not based on how others treat you—but on who God says you are.

- **You are chosen and loved**—*Ephesians* 1:4-5
- **You are made in God's** —*Genesis* 1:27
- **You are not a doormat—you are a temple of the Holy Spirit**—1 *Corinthians* 6:19-20
- **You are valuable**—*Luke* 12:6-7

Setting a boundary is saying, "*I agree with God about my worth.*"

What Are Boundaries?

Boundaries are not barriers to love. They are the gates and fences that protect peace, healing, and truth.

They help you:

- Guard your healing
- Protect your peace
- Keep your heart soft and mind clear
- Invite healthy, godly relationships

Proverbs 4:23 says:

"Above all else, guard your heart, for everything you do flows from it."

Why Boundaries Can Feel Hard

If you've lived through trauma or addiction, boundaries might feel unnatural or unsafe. You may have learned:

- "I don't matter."
- "If I say no, I'll be abandoned."
- "God wants me to forgive and stay quiet."

But the Bible shows something different:

- Jesus walked away from toxic crowds—*Luke 4:28–30*
- God set boundaries in Eden—*Genesis 2:16–17*
- God does not ask us to tolerate evil—*Psalm 11:5; Proverbs 22:3*

How to Set Healthy, God-Honoring Boundaries

Step 1: Ask God what needs protecting—your peace, voice, safety, your children.

Step 2: Use clear, respectful language:

- "I'm not comfortable with that."
- "That doesn't work for me."
- "Please don't speak to me that way."

Step 3: Expect resistance. That doesn't mean your boundary is wrong—it means it's working.

Step 4: Stay connected to God and safe people for strength, clarity, and support.

Why Boundaries Are Loving

Setting a boundary may be the most loving thing you can do—for both of you.

1. It exposes the truth.
2. It creates space for conviction.
3. It reflects the heart of God, who disciplines those He loves (*Hebrews* 12:6).

You're saying:

- *"I love you enough not to let you keep sinning against me."*
- *"I love myself enough to honor the image of God in me."*

You are not selfish. You are walking in truth.

Healthy Boundaries as a Form of Spiritual Growth

Boundaries are not unloving—they are deeply biblical. Dr. Henry Cloud and Dr. John Townsend's book *Boundaries* and Lysa TerKeurst's *Good Boundaries and Goodbyes* teach that boundaries help us steward our relationships, time, and emotional energy with wisdom.

God Himself sets boundaries. He does not tolerate unrepentant sin. He does not allow access without humility. He extends mercy, but never at the cost of His holiness.

As you heal, learning to set boundaries will help you:

- Protect what God is restoring.
- Walk in wisdom, not guilt.
- Love without enabling or losing yourself.

Boundaries are not about shutting people out—they are about opening space for truth, safety, and healthy connection. Boundaries are about love—**often the most loving thing I can do for someone is to have appropriate, consistent boundaries for myself that force that person to recognize that I am a separate and equal person.** My identity is not wrapped up in pleasing them, even if it was in the past. I am now willing to allow that person to experience the consequences of their actions, including no longer giving them the pleasure of my company if that is what it takes.

This creates tension and agitation in a relationship. Lysa TerKeurst said it well: "The tension exists because you are doing the difficult work of no longer cooperating with dysfunction." She also said: "Your light exposes something inside of them they'd rather keep hidden in the darkness. So, of course, it's offensive to them. It's painful to feel exposed." [xviii]

When the Safest Boundary is No Contact

In some cases, the most loving, necessary boundary is **no contact at all**.

This may feel extreme—especially for Christian women who have been taught that grace always means staying open, staying reachable, staying relational. But when someone has consistently abused, manipulated, or retraumatized you, cutting off contact is not cruelty. It's clarity.

It's saying:

"I will no longer give you access to harm me."
"I am choosing safety over sentiment."
"I'm not responsible for your feelings—I'm responsible for my healing."

What No Contact Can Look Like:

- Blocking their number or email.
- Removing them from social media.
- Not responding to messages, even if they appear "nice" or "spiritual."
- Instructing others not to pass along messages or updates from them.
- Avoiding places you know they will be (whenever possible).

Why No Contact Is Hard:

- You may still love the person.
- You may fear what others will think.
- You may feel guilt over "cutting someone off."
- You may have moments of loneliness and longing.
- You may worry that this decision is unchristian.
- You may fear that going no contact will escalate their anger and aggression.

But here's the truth: **God does not call us to stay accessible to destruction.**

Jesus Himself walked away from unsafe people (Luke 4:30). He set limits on access, even among those who claimed to follow Him. Love does not mean staying available to someone who continually violates your boundaries and refuses to repent.

"But what if they've changed?"

Then they can demonstrate that—over time, with consistency, and from a distance.

Trust is rebuilt through actions, not access.

If real change has taken place, one of the first signs will be their willingness to give you space—**without pressure, without demands, and without expectations**. They will accept responsibility for the trust they destroyed and recognize that some relationships may not be fully restored this side of Heaven because of the depth of damage done.

That kind of humility is rare. But it is one of the clearest signs of genuine transformation.

And even then—you do **not** have to be the one to monitor their progress, if any exists at all.

When No Contact Isn't Fully Possible:

In cases where you share children, legal responsibilities, or unavoidable community space, **modified contact** may be the goal. This might include:

- Using a third-party communication app (like OurFamilyWizard or Talking Parents).
- Establishing clear communication boundaries through legal agreements.
- Speaking only through attorneys or advocates.

In these cases, the principle is the same: **less emotional access, more protective structure**. You are not obligated to have vulnerable or personal conversations with someone who has proven unsafe. You are allowed to guard your heart—even in shared spaces.

It is beyond the scope of this book to go deeply into co-parenting vs parallel parenting, but there are good resources such as Wilderness to Wild and Called To Peace Ministries advocacy services that can help you navigate these tough issues.

Red Flags for Boundary Violations in Relationships

Boundaries aren't just theory. Violations show up in very real and painful ways. If any of these patterns are showing up in your relationship, pay attention. These are not "normal" rough patches. They may indicate emotional, spiritual, or psychological abuse.

Emotional & Psychological

- Guilt-tripping or manipulation when you say no.
- "Love bombing" or pushing for intense emotional closeness early.
- Dismissing your feelings or calling you too sensitive.
- Demanding access to your private accounts or location.
- Blaming you for their emotions ("You made me angry").

- Controlling who you see or talk to.

Physical & Sexual

- Ignoring your limits or boundaries with touch.
- Pressuring sexual activity when you're not ready.
- Using affection as a bargaining tool.
- Not accepting "no" the first time.
- Touching you in anger or without consent.

Spiritual & Identity

- Using Scripture to control or shame you.
- Mocking or minimizing your beliefs.
- Insisting their interpretation of faith is the only right one.
- Treating spiritual authority as power over you.

Time, Space & Communication

- Showing up uninvited.
- Expecting constant contact or instant replies.
- Getting angry when you need space or silence.
- Pressuring you to resolve conflict before you're ready.

Financial & Life Decisions

- Controlling your spending.
- Pressuring life decisions before you're ready.
- Expecting you to sacrifice dreams or independence.
- Keeping financial secrets or demanding full control prematurely.

Accountability & Respect

- Twisting your words or denying past actions (gaslighting).
- Always blaming others.
- Refusing to apologize.
- Mocking your boundaries as "selfish" or "unbiblical."
- Retaliating when you set a boundary.
- Repeating behaviors even after being told "no."

Chapter 14 Reflection and Application—Where Do I Need Boundaries?

Take a moment to reflect with God. These questions are designed to help you recognize red flags, uncover beliefs that may be holding you back, and discern where healthy, loving boundaries are needed in your life and relationships.

Emotional & Psychological Boundaries

- Have I felt guilty or pressured for saying "no"? How did the other person respond?
- Have I been told I'm too sensitive or had my feelings dismissed?
- Have I been blamed for someone else's emotions or reactions?
- Are there relationships where I feel like I'm always walking on eggshells?

Physical & Sexual Boundaries

- Have I been touched in a way that made me uncomfortable—even after speaking up?
- Have I felt pressured to be physically or sexually affectionate before I was ready?
- How does my partner respond when I express a physical or sexual boundary?

Spiritual & Identity Boundaries

- Have I been controlled or shamed using Scripture or religious language?
- Have my beliefs or convictions ever been mocked, dismissed, or ignored?

- Do I feel free to grow spiritually in this relationship, or do I feel stifled or afraid?

Time, Space, & Communication Boundaries

- Can I take time for myself without guilt or backlash?
- Are there unhealthy expectations around instant replies or constant contact?
- During conflict, am I allowed space to process—or am I pressured to engage before I'm ready?

Financial & Life Decision Boundaries

- Have I been criticized or controlled around how I spend money or time?
- Have I been pressured into major decisions before I felt ready?
- Is there mutual respect and transparency around financial matters?

Accountability & Respect Boundaries

- When someone hurts me, do they take responsibility—or shift the blame?

- Have I been made to question my memory or version of events?
- What happens when I express a boundary—am I respected, ignored, or punished?

Personal Heart Check

- What lie have I believed that kept me from setting boundaries?
- Where is God asking me to guard my heart more intentionally?
- Which boundary red flags stood out to me the most—and why?
- Have I ever justified or ignored a red flag? What were the consequences?
- What steps can I take to protect and honor my boundaries moving forward?
- Who are the safe people I can talk to when I feel uncertain, overwhelmed, or unsafe?

Chapter 15:

WHEN THE CHURCH FAILS TO PROTECT AND VALUE WOMEN

Introduction: Naming the Betrayal

For a long time, she thought the church was the safest place she could go.

She sat trembling in her pastor's office, hands wrapped tightly around a cup of lukewarm coffee, pouring out the truth she had been too afraid to name for years.

She told him about the emotional blowups. The long stretches of silent punishment. The threats. The outbursts. The growing signs that her husband, once celebrated for his sobriety, was sliding back into old addictions—or at least old patterns.

She waited for comfort. For clarity. For someone to stand beside her.

But what she got was something very different.

- *Are you sure you're not exaggerating?*

- **Maybe if you focus on being more forgiving, he'll feel safe to open up.**
- **Marriage is hard for everyone—we all bring our baggage.**
- **You need to submit more and respect him, even when it's hard.**
- **Have you been meeting his physical needs? Maybe if you're more available sexually, he'll come around.**
- **God hates divorce, sister. Let's work on reconciliation.**

She left the office not relieved but crushed.
Alone.
Spiritually shamed.
Unseen.

This story isn't rare.

It's repeated in countless variations across churches of all sizes, denominations, and countries. Women come forward, trembling, vulnerable, sometimes even terrified—and instead of protection, they are met with suspicion, minimization, or blame.

Before we can talk about how the Church can be a safe haven—a refuge, a place of justice and truth—we have to face the heartbreaking reality that far too often it has been the opposite.

The Church is called to reflect the heart of Christ: to protect the oppressed, confront the sinner, and lift up the brokenhearted. But when it prioritizes appearance over truth, control over humility, or male leadership over female dignity, it becomes complicit in the very abuse it should be opposing.

People in the church can become "flying monkeys" (Wizard of Oz) for the abuser, whether they understand what they are doing or not.

This chapter is not an attack on the Body of Christ. It is a lament. It is an honest reckoning. And it is a necessary step if we are to clear away the rubble and rebuild something true.

Because the Church is not meant to be a place of shame. It is meant to be the sheltering arms of Jesus Himself.

"Pastors and church leaders must get this right. People's lives are at stake."[xix]

Neil Schori

The Idol of Appearance Over Truth

For some churches, the greatest threat is not sin—it's scandal.

They say they want truth.

They say they want healing.

They say they want repentance.

But when the truth threatens the image of the church, the reputation of a leader, or the comfort of the congregation, far too many quietly choose appearance over accountability. This is not a new problem. In Matthew 23, Jesus rebuked the religious leaders of His day, saying:

"Woe to you, teachers of the law and Pharisees, you hypocrites! You are like whitewashed tombs, which look beautiful on the

outside but on the inside are full of the bones of the dead and everything unclean." (v. 27)

They worked tirelessly to keep things looking righteous on the outside, while inside, rot and death were spreading. It wasn't just an individual failure—it was a system-wide, institutional failure.

"Too often, the church's response to abuse and inequity reveals a painful truth: that protecting systems has taken precedence over protecting people."[xx]

What Appearance-Over-Truth Looks Like Today:

- Church leaders dismiss or downplay abuse reports to "protect the ministry's reputation."
- Congregations rally around a charismatic abuser because "he's done so much good work."
- Elders silence victims to avoid legal complications or media attention.
- Denominational heads look the other way because "he's family," "he's anointed," or "God is using him."

The underlying message is clear:

It's not the sin that destroys—it's the exposure of the sin.

This leads some churches to cover up abuse, excuse harmful patterns, and rush to "move on" before real accountability has happened. Survivors are told they're divisive or unforgiving for simply speaking the truth. In some cases, they're pressured to leave, while the abuser is quietly kept or even promoted.

The Cost of Protecting the System:

When the system is protected over the individual, the Body of Christ fractures. Women and children leave—often in silence and grief—feeling that the church has betrayed them.

And worse, the name of Jesus is profaned.

Cover-ups don't just damage victims.

They damage the witness of the Church to the world.

They tell the watching world:

- We *value reputation more than repentance.*
- We *value comfort more than justice.*
- We *value power more than truth.*

This is not the gospel. Wade Mullen said:

"There are two basic paths: adopt truth-telling and transparency, regardless of the impact on one's legitimacy, status, or image; or use impression management and public relation strategies intended to portray and protect legitimacy, status, and a positive image."[xxi]

The Church's Role in Escalation Risk

It must be said: **when churches pressure women to return or delay leaving for the sake of "peace," they are increasing her risk.** Many women are retraumatized when spiritual leaders dismiss their safety concerns or push reconciliation before there is true repentance.

God does not call women to die on the altar of their husband's sin. He calls us to walk in wisdom—and to protect life.

> *"The prudent see danger and take refuge, but the simple keep going and pay the penalty" (Proverbs 22:3)*

If you are afraid of retaliation, it does not mean you're weak. It means you've been surviving something deadly serious. And now, you are choosing to step into the light with both courage and caution.

You are not alone.

> *"Being able to 'just leave' an abusive relationship or situation is very often the exception, not the rule."*[xxii]

> *Glenn Patrick Doyle*

Misusing Theology to Silence Women

When a woman reaches the breaking point and speaks up about abuse, addiction, or betrayal in her marriage, she often faces not just relational pushback—but theological pushback.

It sounds spiritual.

It's framed as biblical.

But in practice, it's often a distortion of God's Word that keeps women bound in harmful, even dangerous situations.

Submission Misapplied:

Yes, Scripture calls wives to submit to their husbands (Ephesians 5:22).

But it also calls husbands to love their wives as Christ loved the church (Ephesians 5:25) — sacrificially, protectively, servant-heartedly. Just one verse before Ephesians 5:22, Paul gives this command:

"Submit to one another out of reverence for Christ." *(Ephesians 5:21)*

Submission was never designed to be one-sided domination. It was meant to be mutual, Christ-centered, and love-filled.

The concept of headship (*kephalē*) is also often misunderstood. In context, it carries the sense of source or origin—not tyrannical authority. Christ's headship over the church is marked by sacrifice, humility, and service—not coercion or entitlement. When submission is taught in isolation, without the balance of mutual accountability and Christlike love, it becomes a weapon.

Submission and Headship: A Closer Look

Much has been written—and weaponized—about the concepts of *submission* and *headship* in Christian marriage. For many women in abusive marriages, these words have been used to pressure them into silence and endurance, often under the mistaken belief that suffering under oppression somehow honors God. But what do these words actually mean in Scripture?

Biblical scholar and ancient language expert Marg Mowczko has done extensive work unpacking these ideas. She notes that the Greek word *kephalē* (translated as "head") has often been assumed to mean *leader* or *authority*, but that's not how it was commonly used in first-century Greek. In fact, she explains that *kephalē* more often carried the meaning of *source*—as in the head of a river—or the beginning or origin of something.[xxiii]

When Paul writes in Ephesians 5:23, "*For the husband is the head of the wife as Christ is the head of the church, his body, of which he is the Savior,*" he is not giving husbands a divine right to rule over their wives. Marg points out that Paul redefines *headship* here in light of Jesus, who gave himself up sacrificially, humbly, for the good of his people. Christ's headship is expressed in servanthood, not domination.

Furthermore, the **mutual submission** called for in Ephesians 5:21—"*Submit to one another out of reverence for Christ*"—sets the stage for everything that follows. The wife's submission is not a one-sided command; both husband and wife are called to submit, to serve, and to love one another. Marg writes that the entire household code in Ephesians was radically softened by Paul's emphasis on Christlike love and humility, directly challenging the harsh patriarchal norms of Roman culture.[xxiv]

It's also worth noting that biblical submission is never framed as permission for abuse. As Mowczko points out, submission in Scripture is something a person offers freely, not something that can be demanded or coerced. A husband trying to *force* his wife to submit is already outside the spirit of the gospel—he is called to lay down his life, not exert power over her.

Marg also emphasizes that the New Testament's household instructions were contextual, addressing specific social structures of the time, but they were infused with kingdom values that elevated the dignity of women, children, and slaves far beyond what Roman law required. Paul's words do not endorse hierarchy or control; rather, they call believers to live out the self-giving love of Jesus.[xxv]

In abusive marriages, the pattern we see is the opposite of Christlike headship: instead of sacrificial love, there is domination; instead of mutuality, there is control; instead of nurturing, there is harm. Scripture never tells women to submit to sin or violence. To do so would dishonor both the wife and the image of God in her.

Forgiveness Misunderstood:

Women are often pressured to "forgive and forget"—to reconcile and trust again without evidence of real change.

They hear:

- *You need to forgive seventy times seven.*
- *Don't keep a record of wrongs—love covers a multitude of sins.*
- *We're all sinners; who are you to withhold forgiveness?*

But biblical forgiveness never bypasses truth or erases accountability. Forgiveness can be freely given, as an act of the heart. Reconciliation, however, must be earned, as an act of trust.

Loving the False Redemption Story

There's something deeply beautiful about the gospel:

We serve a God who redeems.

Who restores.

Who takes the worst failures and makes them new.

But the beauty of redemption has a dark side when churches fall in love with the *story* of redemption more than the *truth* of repentance.

The Danger of Performative Repentance:

Abusers are often masterful performers. They know how to cry at the right moment, confess just enough, and tell a dramatic "before-and-after" story.

Churches, eager to celebrate transformation, quickly place these men on platforms, share their testimonies, and praise their "turnaround"—sometimes after only weeks or months.

Meanwhile, the woman who lives the daily reality of the abuse is left wondering:

- *Why is no one asking if the change is real?*
- *Why am I called bitter for pointing out ongoing harm?*
- *Why am I losing my church community while he's gaining applause?*

Why the Church Falls for the Show

Churches often fall into this trap because:

1. They want a good story. A dramatic testimony of freedom from addiction is powerful, marketable, and inspiring.
2. They are uncomfortable with ongoing accountability. Long-term change requires long-term work, and many churches want to believe a quick apology is enough.
3. They are more familiar with the abuser. In many cases, the man has deep relational ties, leadership roles, or

public influence in the church—while the woman's concerns feel like a threat to stability.

In this context, the church's hunger for a "success story" can become more important than the survivor's safety, healing, or voice.

Biblical Repentance Takes Time:

True repentance is not a moment: it's a process.

It's not measured by tears; it's measured by time and consistency.

It's not about appearing transformed; it's about becoming transformed.

When churches rush to proclaim a redemption story without real accountability, they risk becoming complicit in ongoing harm.

Failing in Discipleship and Leadership Accountability

When churches mishandle abuse, it's not just a failure to protect women—it's a failure of discipleship. At its core, discipleship is about becoming more like Christ:

- Humble.
- Teachable.
- Accountable.
- Willing to die to self.

But when abusive or addicted men are given repeated chances without deep, ongoing discipleship, the church is not helping them become Christlike—it's enabling sin.

When Leadership Prioritizes Gifts Over Character:

In many churches, outward success is prized:

- Does he teach well?
- Does he lead well?
- Does he tithe well?

When a man has gifts or influence, the temptation is to minimize his sins to preserve his usefulness. But Scripture is clear: church leaders must be above reproach, gentle, faithful, and self-controlled (1 Timothy 3; Titus 1).

Ignoring these standards does not extend grace—it corrupts it.

The Absence of Women's Voices:

When decision-making tables are filled only with men, especially men unfamiliar with trauma or abuse dynamics, blind spots multiply.

Women's voices are not a threat to the gospel.

They are a gift to the body.

When churches fail to listen, they silence not just women—they silence the Spirit, who pours out His gifts on sons and daughters alike (Acts 2:17).

The Impact on Women and Families

When the church fails to protect women and confront abusive men, the fallout ripples outward.

Isolation and Spiritual Abandonment:

For many women, the deepest wound is not what their husband did—it's how the church responded.

They come seeking refuge and are met with suspicion.

They come seeking truth and are met with minimization.

They come seeking justice and are met with spiritual pressure to endure.

Some leave the church, not because they are walking away from Christ, but because they no longer feel safe in His house. Others stay but live with a deep, unnamed ache, feeling they are second-class citizens in the kingdom.

The Toll on Children:

Children are often the silent casualties.

They watch their mother be silenced. They watch their father avoid accountability. They learn that church is a place where appearances matter more than truth, where power goes unchecked, and where pain is hidden.

Unless the cycle is broken, many grow up to replicate the same patterns—either as future victims or future abusers.

The Witness of the Church:

When the church mishandles abuse, the watching world sees a false picture of Christ. Instead of reflecting the God who defends the oppressed, it looks like an institution that protects abusers.

Instead of showcasing the gospel of freedom, it showcases a system of cover-up and control.

This is not a small failure.

This is a gospel failure.

"Woe to you... You shut the door of the kingdom of heaven in people's faces." (Matthew 23:13)

A Heart That Grieves

If you are a survivor reading this:

You are not alone.

You are not the problem.

You are not forgotten by God.

He sees.

He knows.

And He grieves over the way His church has failed you.

Conclusion: The Heart of Jesus Is Not Reflected Here

The failures named in this chapter are heavy—and they should be.

But hear this clearly: **these failures are not the heart of Christ.**

Jesus does not silence the hurting.

Jesus does not cover up sin to preserve appearances.

Jesus does not send abused women back into danger or blame them for the harm done to them.

Jesus does not minimize addiction, abuse, or betrayal.

And Jesus does not use Scripture as a whip to drive wounded people into deeper bondage.

When the church fails to protect and value women, it betrays not just those women—it betrays the very gospel it claims to preach.

But that is not where the story ends.

There are churches—often quiet, humble, sometimes small— where the heart of Jesus beats strong.

Where the broken are believed.

Where the oppressed are defended.

Where men are called to repentance with clarity and courage.

Where women are seen, honored, and sheltered.

These churches exist.

They may not make headlines.

They may not draw crowds.

But they shine with the beauty of Christ.

Neil Schori, of Called to Peace Ministries, said: "*If each and every American church designated five 'safe families' to give victims temporary shelters, we could literally rescue every single woman who would be abused this year.*[xxvi]

Churches can make a major difference in the safety, healing, and hope that a woman leaving an abusive relationship can have. We need to be a very practical light in a very dark world.

In the next chapter, we will explore what it looks like when the Church becomes a safe haven— when it steps into its true calling as the Body of Christ, the refuge for the weary, the defender of the oppressed, and the living witness of God's justice and mercy on earth.

There is hope.

And there is a remnant.

Let's go find it.

Chapter 15 Discussion Questions

1. **Naming the Betrayal**

   Think of a time you sought help from a church leader. What response did you receive, and how did it shape your trust in the church—or in God?

2. **Appearance Over Truth**

   Have you seen a church choose image or reputation over accountability? How did that decision affect the people who were hurting?

3. **Misused Scripture**

   Which biblical passage has been weaponized against you (or someone you know) to silence abuse? How does its true context change your understanding?

4. **Submission Re-examined**

   After reading the deeper look at *kephalē* and mutual submission, how would you explain biblical headship to someone who sees it as license for control?

5. **Forgiveness vs. Reconciliation**

   Describe a time you felt pressured to forgive quickly or "move on." What boundaries or steps would genuine, healthy reconciliation require instead?

6. **The Allure of a Redemption Story**

   Why do you think churches are so eager to spotlight rapid "turnarounds"? How can we celebrate repentance without minimizing the victim's safety and healing?

7. **Leadership Blind Spots**

   How has the absence of women's voices in decision-making affected abuse responses you've witnessed? What practical change would broaden perspective?

8. **Personal Fallout**

   In what ways has a mishandled church response impacted your faith, self-worth, or view of community? What has helped—or could help—you begin to heal?

9. **Protecting the Vulnerable**

   Proverbs 31:8 commands us to "speak up for those who cannot speak for themselves." What would speaking up look like in your current context?

10. **Finding the Remnant**

    The chapter ends with hope that safe, justice-seeking churches exist. What qualities will you look for—and which non-negotiables will you require—as you seek a healthy faith community?

Chapter 16:

THE CHURCH AS A SAFE HAVEN

Introduction: A Vision of Hope

She sat in the back row, trembling.

It had taken everything in her to step inside the church that morning. After months of isolation, after countless nights crying on the bathroom floor, after leaving behind a marriage marked by control, addiction, and emotional harm—she wondered if there was any place left for her in God's house.

She didn't expect what happened next.

The pastor, a quiet man she had never met, came and sat beside her. He didn't ask invasive questions. He didn't offer pat answers. He simply said: "I want you to know you're safe here. You are believed. And you are welcome."

When she asked for help, they didn't send her back home or question her story. They helped her find housing. They provided counseling referrals. They prayed with her and for her, without agenda or pressure.

When her abuser showed up, demanding access and spinning a polished story, the elders stood firm. They protected her—and her children—from further harm.

This was the church she feared she would never find. This was the heart of Christ, made visible.

The Good News

Not every church gets it wrong. Not every pastor minimizes harm. Not every Christian community rushes to reconciliation without repentance.

There *are* churches that walk in the light. There *are* churches that stand up for the oppressed.

There *are* churches that reflect the heart of Jesus: full of truth, justice, mercy, and love.

This chapter is about those churches.

It's about what the church can be—and what, by God's grace, many are already becoming.

Characteristics of a Safe Church

What does a safe, Christ-honoring church look like?

It's not about size, denomination, or worship style. It's about culture. It's about character.

It's about the collective heart of the people who claim the name of Jesus.

Here are some defining marks of a safe, redemptive church:

Truth-Telling

A safe church walks in the light. It does not cover sin to protect reputation. It does not silence victims to maintain comfort. It does not pretend that darkness doesn't exist in its midst.

Instead, it listens carefully. It investigates thoroughly. It names sin clearly—no matter who is involved or how inconvenient it may be. Just because a man is a pastor or is on the pastoral staff doesn't guarantee that he is a safe person behind closed doors. Sarah McDugal of Wilderness to Wild ministry is an example of a woman who was the wife of a very abusive pastor for many years. A pastor's wife who exposes her husband's evil often loses her community, his income, and sometimes the home they were living in (parsonage). Churches need to support her with intentionality and deep, long-lasting support.

> "Have nothing to do with the fruitless deeds of darkness, but rather expose them." (Ephesians 5:11)

In a safe church, no one is above correction. It doesn't matter how gifted, charismatic, or beloved a leader or member is— their actions are measured against the standard of Scripture, not popularity. There are clear policies in place:

- Leaders are held to the highest standards of integrity.

- Reports of abuse are taken seriously and investigated promptly.
- Abusers are removed from positions of influence, not protected or platformed.

This is not cruelty. This is love—love for the flock, love for truth, and even love for the one caught in sin, who must face consequences in order to truly repent.

Abuse and Trauma-Informed Care

A safe church doesn't just quote Bible verses at wounded people—it seeks to understand the wounds. Leaders are trained to recognize the effects of trauma, abuse, addiction, and coercive control. They know how to respond wisely, not reactively. They prioritize safety over appearances, understanding that survivors often carry layers of fear, shame, and confusion that cannot be swept away with quick spiritual answers.

There are ministries that offer training in trauma-informed care and advocacy, such as Called to Peace Ministries, Wilderness to Wild, and Give Her Wings Academy. There is also a robust abuse support community that is providing training for church leaders as well as lay members of the church community.

Protection of the Vulnerable

Jesus consistently centered the vulnerable—women, children, the poor, the marginalized. A safe church does the same.

It creates space for survivors to speak.

It provides resources for those in crisis.

It refuses to let the powerful overshadow the powerless.

This is not because the vulnerable are more important than others—it's because they are the ones most easily silenced or forgotten.

Humility and Shared Leadership

A safe church does not pretend to know everything. It asks for help. It learns from experts. It invites women's voices into decision-making, recognizing that the body of Christ is made up of both sons and daughters (Acts 2:17). It is humble enough to admit when it has failed—and courageous enough to change.

What Survivors Need from Their Churches

For a woman who has walked through abuse, addiction, betrayal, or abandonment, stepping through the doors of her church can feel like stepping onto a minefield. She's not just carrying spiritual wounds. She's carrying trauma, fear, grief, and often a profound sense of spiritual confusion: *"Where is God in all of this? Where is His body, the Church, when I need shelter?"*

When she reaches out, what she needs from her church is not perfection. She knows no community is perfect.

What she needs is protection.

What she needs is belonging.

What she needs is clarity that she is seen, valued, and safe.

She needs to be believed and taken seriously.

The first wound most survivors face is disbelief.

- *"Are you sure you're not exaggerating?"*
- *"You seem bitter — have you forgiven?"*
- *"Maybe you're both just struggling and need counseling."*

A safe church listens carefully, takes her seriously, and does not require her to prove her pain before offering help.

She needs to be protected, not blamed

This is where many churches fail.

Too often, the abuser is allowed to remain fully present in the church community—attending services, volunteering, even serving in leadership—while the survivor is left navigating triggers, fear, and spiritual displacement. A woman cannot heal in a place where she is constantly re-exposed to the presence and power of the one who harmed her.

Even if legal or church discipline processes are still ongoing, a safe church will take practical steps to shield the survivor from unnecessary contact and emotional harm. This might mean asking the abuser to step away from the congregation, limiting his access to shared spaces, or providing alternative service times or ministry settings. If the church suggests alternative service times, they should be sure to enforce those, especially when the wife has gone "no contact" with her abuser.

To stand with the vulnerable means centering their safety, not preserving the comfort or reputation of the one who caused harm.

When a church fails to protect the survivor, it sends a loud, unspoken message: *"You are less valuable to us than he is."* That is a deep wound—and one that many women carry for years. This is personal to me. Some of the deepest and most unexpected wounds I experienced were from my former church leadership.

Churches who have supported the family while the husband was in addiction rehab and have embraced his public testimony afterwards may feel that they have "egg on their face" when the wife finally gets the courage to report what is going on. The temptation is to maintain the public persona of the abuser rather than deal compassionately with the wife.

She Needs Spiritual and Practical Support

She doesn't just need Bible verses or prayer. She needs real, tangible help:

- Counseling referrals.
- Help with housing or childcare.
- Financial aid, if needed.
- Pastoral and elder support that is informed, compassionate, and clear-eyed about the dynamics of abuse.

She Needs Space to Heal Without Pressure

She needs time. Time to grieve. Time to process. Time to rediscover her voice and her faith apart from manipulation. A safe church doesn't pressure her to "forgive and forget," to reconcile, or to return to her abuser prematurely (or at all). It gives her room to breathe and trusts God's timeline, not the church's convenience.

How Churches Can Equip Themselves

A safe church doesn't happen by accident. It's not just about having "good intentions" or "loving people well." It requires intentional learning, humble listening, and active change.

Many pastors and ministry leaders genuinely want to help but simply don't know how. They weren't trained to recognize abuse. They were taught simplistic views of forgiveness, reconciliation, and authority. They've never heard of trauma-informed ministry or coercive control.

The good news is they don't have to figure it out alone.

Organizations and Leaders Offering Biblical, Trauma-Informed Training

Here are just a few trusted voices offering practical, biblically grounded resources to help churches become places of safety, truth, and healing:

- Psalm 82 Initiative—A faith-based ministry focused on helping churches recognize abuse, confront sin, and protect the vulnerable within their congregations.
- Andrew Bauman—A Christian therapist and author whose work addresses male entitlement, abuse, and trauma recovery; his new book *Safe Church* is designed specifically to help churches assess and strengthen their response to abuse.
- Called to Peace Ministries (Joy Forrest)—A robust ministry supporting both survivors and churches, offering training, advocacy and biblical education on domestic violence and abuse.
- Sarah McDugal / Wilderness to Wild—Focused on exposing toxic Christian culture, equipping women to break free from abuse, and training communities to develop spiritually safe environments.

- GRACE—Godly Response to Abuse in the Christian Environment, www.netgrace.org.
- Church Cares—churchcares.com. This organization offers training for churches seeking to become safe places for those experiencing abuse.
- Focus Ministries— https://www.focusministries1.org/ This includes training for leaders as well as support groups and financial help for women seeking to leave abusive relationships. (Please note that this is **not** Focus on the Family)
- Darby Strickland— *Darbystrickland*.com. Darby offers excellent teaching for church leaders regarding abuse.

This is by no means an exhaustive list but offers good places to start the journey of becoming an abuse-informed safe church or organization.

Investing in Long-Term Change

One sermon won't fix this. One workshop won't solve it. Churches need to commit to long-term learning:

- Training pastors, elders, small group leaders, and staff.
- Creating clear policies for reporting and addressing abuse.
- Establishing accountability systems for leadership.
- Building relationships with local domestic violence organizations or counselors.

The call of the Church is not just to avoid harm—it's to actively seek justice, protect the vulnerable, and reflect the heart of Christ in every part of its life together.

Real-Life Examples of Redemptive Church Responses

It's easy to become discouraged when we hear story after story of church failure, but that is not the whole story. There are churches, pastors, elders, and faith communities who are getting this right.

Sometimes they're small rural congregations; sometimes they're urban churches with dedicated pastoral care teams. What unites them is not their size or fame but their commitment to **walk in the way of Christ** by protecting the vulnerable, standing for truth, and pursuing justice.

Here are just a few examples drawn from real survivor accounts and composite stories:

A Pastor Who Listened and Believed

When Anna came forward to her church leadership about her husband's increasing rage, control, and hidden addiction, she braced herself for minimization. But instead, the pastor sat quietly, listened carefully, and said:

"I believe you. You were right to speak up. You are not alone."

He didn't rush her into reconciliation. He helped her find safe housing. He connected her with trauma-informed counselors. He involved the elder board to confront her husband and make clear that accountability—not appearances—was the church's priority.

A Church That Took Clear Action
When reports surfaced about a prominent church volunteer abusing his wife Alicia, the elders acted quickly. They immediately removed him from leadership. They worked with outside professionals to investigate the situation.

They provided ongoing support for Alicia, including practical resources, prayer, and regular check-ins. They didn't platform the abuser's public apology or pressure the couple to reconcile. Instead, they focused on safety, truth, and healing—for everyone involved.

A Congregation That Wrapped Around a Survivor
When Lisa's marriage ended after years of hidden abuse, she feared becoming invisible in her church community. But her church family surprised her. Women's ministry leaders offered to babysit when she needed space to grieve. Small group members provided meals and financial help during the divorce. Pastoral staff regularly reminded her that she was valued, loved, and fully welcomed—not marked or shamed by her marital status.

This church didn't just speak words of comfort—they became the hands and feet of Christ.

These examples are not fiction. They reflect what the Church can be—and what, by God's grace, more and more churches are becoming.

For Further Discernment

Abuse in Christian marriages—especially where addiction recovery is part of the story—can remain hidden behind public sobriety and spiritual language. If you are a pastor, ministry leader, or women's ministry volunteer, I encourage you to review the checklist provided in **Appendix A: Recognizing Hidden Abuse in the Church**. It offers practical insight to help you notice red flags and gently support women who may be suffering in silence. Sometimes the ones who look the most committed are the ones in the deepest pain.

Conclusion: The Remnant Church

There is a remnant.

Even in a time when many churches have failed to protect the vulnerable...

Even in a time when too many pulpits have prioritized power over people...

Even when survivors carry wounds not only from their marriages but from the very place meant to be their spiritual refuge...

There is still a remnant.

There are churches who love the heart of Christ more than the appearance of success.

There are pastors who lay down their own egos to stand beside the hurting.

There are elders who uphold justice with clarity and conviction.

There are congregations who choose the slow, holy work of walking with survivors through long seasons of healing.

These are the places where the Body of Christ shines. These are the places where the weary find rest, the wounded find shelter, and the brokenhearted find a new beginning.

If you are a survivor reading this: **do not give up hope.**

Not every church will fail you.

Not every Christian community will look like the one you left behind.

God's people are still alive, still rising, still reflecting His heart—even if you have to search and sift to find them.

"So I will restore to you the years that the swarming locust has eaten." (Joel 2:25, NKJV)

There is a place for you in the Body of Christ.

There is a place where you are seen, protected, and valued.

There is a place where the Church becomes what it was always meant to be: a safe haven.

Chapter 16 Discussion Questions

1. **A Church That Protects**

   Have you ever encountered a church—or even one person in a church—that made you feel genuinely safe, believed, and supported? What stood out about how they responded?

2. **Truth-Telling Culture**

   What does it look like, in your experience, when a church chooses *truth over image*? What might a church risk or sacrifice to walk in that kind of integrity?

3. **Being Trauma-Informed**

   How would you explain the difference between a church that is well-meaning and one that is trauma-informed? Why is that distinction so important for survivors?

4. **Protection vs. Platform**

   This chapter describes how abusers are sometimes platformed while survivors are sidelined. Why do you think this happens, and what do you believe a truly protective church should do instead?

5. **The Role of Humility**

   How does shared leadership—including the presence and voices of women—help prevent the blind spots that often lead to mishandling abuse?

6. **Rebuilding Trust After Church Harm**

   If you've been hurt by a church in the past, what

are some signs you would look for now in a faith community that might be safe and restorative?

7. **Support That Goes Beyond Prayer**

   What forms of **practical help** (housing, finances, childcare, etc.) might a church provide to a woman in crisis? What would it mean for a survivor to receive that help without shame?

8. **Time and Space to Heal**

   Why is it harmful when churches pressure women to forgive quickly or reconcile prematurely? What could it look like for a church to honor a survivor's healing timeline?

9. **Learning and Unlearning**

   This chapter names the need for long-term training and education. What do you think most churches need to *unlearn* about abuse, and what do they most need to *learn*?

10. **Finding the Remnant**

    The chapter ends with a message of hope: that there are still churches living out the heart of Christ. How does that truth encourage you today? What do you need to believe again about the possibility of a safe, Christ-honoring community?

Chapter 17:

REBUILDING LIFE IN CHRIST

Introduction: A New Beginning

You are surviving what you thought might break you.

You have walked through the valley of betrayal, abuse, loss, and grief.

You have faced the hard truths, set the hard boundaries, and made choices that cost you deeply.

And now, you stand here—on the edge of something new.

This chapter is not about erasing the past.

It's about stepping into the future: a life rebuilt not on fear, shame, or survival, but on the unshakable foundation of who you are in Christ.

You are not just a woman who left.

You are not just a survivor of abuse.

You are a beloved daughter of God, clothed in the righteousness of Jesus, held in the arms of El Roi, the God who sees.

This is your invitation: to come and rebuild—gently, slowly, intentionally—and to let the One who loves you best restore what was lost.

Remembering Who You Are—Identity in Christ

The voices of abuse linger long after the relationship ends.

- "You're worthless."
- "You're not enough."
- "You're a failure as a wife, a mother, a Christian."

Even if your abuser is no longer speaking those words, they often echo in your own mind, tangled up with years of pain and spiritual confusion.

But here is the truth:

You are not defined by what was done to you.

You are not defined by the failure of your marriage, the opinions of your church, or even your own moments of weakness.

You are defined by Christ.

"God made Him who had no sin to be sin for us, so that
in Him we might become the righteousness of God."
(2 Corinthians 5:21)

When God looks at you, He sees you covered in the righteousness of Jesus—chosen, beloved, redeemed. You are adopted into His family (Ephesians 1:5), made new (2 Corinthians 5:17), and held securely in His love (Romans 8:38–39).

Healing is not about striving harder to fix ourselves—it's about abiding in Christ, resting in His finished work, and letting His love transform the deep places of our hearts.

Healing From Trauma—Spirit, Soul, and Body

Healing is not just emotional. It touches every part of who you are—because God made you as a whole, integrated being:

- **Spirit**—the eternal part of you, already seated with Christ in the heavenly realms (Ephesians 2:6).
- **Soul**—your mind, will, and emotions, the battleground where healing and transformation unfold.
- **Body**—your physical self, where trauma often leaves marks long after the events have passed.

While your spirit is already secure in Christ, your soul and body need time, care, and patience to heal. This may involve trauma-informed counseling, gentle spiritual practices, physical rest, and learning to quiet the lies of the past and receive God's truth in new ways.

Remember: healing is not a straight line, and you do not walk it alone. The Good Shepherd restores your soul, one step at a time (Psalm 23:3).

The Healing Power of Connection: Finding Your Tribe

Healing from abuse is not meant to be a solitary journey. God created us for connection. From the Garden of Eden to the early church, Scripture shows us the importance of relationship, community, and shared burdens.

Abuse isolates—it cuts us off from others and even from ourselves. So, healing must be relational. The harm began in the context of relationship, and restoration often comes through safe, supportive relationships.

Lia didn't think she needed connection at first.

After years of walking on eggshells in her marriage, she had finally stepped away—only to discover that the silence on the other side felt just as heavy. She had her Bible, her journal, and her counselor. But something was still missing.

One night, after another wave of shame hit her out of nowhere, she signed up for a faith-based online support group a friend had gently recommended. She logged in with trembling hands and a hesitant heart, expecting to feel out of place.

Instead, she found women who understood.

They didn't flinch at her story. They didn't rush to fix her. They didn't tell her to go back and try harder.

They listened. They nodded. They spoke truth with tenderness—the kind she hadn't heard in years.

Over time, those women became her lifeline. In their company, she began to believe that she wasn't crazy. That God hadn't abandoned her. That boundaries were not rebellion. That healing was not only possible—it was already beginning.

She still remembers the first time she laughed during one of their Zoom calls. It startled her—joy had become such a foreign thing. But that sacred joy, born in the presence of safe, faith-filled women, was a seed of restoration.

In safe, loving community:

- We begin to rewrite the lies we've believed about ourselves.
- Our nervous systems begin to calm in the presence of safe people.
- We witness others walk in truth, which gives us courage to do the same.

You were never meant to heal alone. You were never meant to carry this burden in isolation. Whether your healing community is in a church small group, a trauma-informed support circle, or a private online space—the key is this: you need others who speak truth, offer compassion, and walk alongside you.

Some of the groups that offer this kind of connection for women of faith include:

Natalie Hoffman's Flying Free Kaleidoscope—for Christian women healing from emotionally and spiritually abusive marriages.

Helena Knowlton's Arise— offering trauma recovery education and support for women of faith.

Leslie Vernick's Conquer Group—a biblically based support group for women in destructive marriages.

Heather Elizabeth's Held and Healed—a community for faith-based healing from abuse and divorce.

> Scripture reminds us: "*Carry each other's burdens, and in this way you will fulfill the law of Christ*" (*Galatians 6:2*). Connection isn't just helpful—it's holy.

Let the lie of isolation die here. Let your heart begin to trust again, little by little, surrounded by others who will hold space for your pain and cheer you on in your healing.

Opportunities for Spiritual Growth and Renewal

Healing isn't just about leaving something behind—it's about discovering what God is calling you toward.

This might include:

- Deepening your prayer life.
- Reading Scripture through the lens of God's love for the oppressed.
- Finding safe, supportive spiritual community.
- Exploring long-buried gifts, callings, or passions.

If You Are Still in the Abusive Situation

If you are reading this and you are still living inside the storm, I want you to hear this clearly:

You are seen.

You are valuable.

You are not forgotten by God.

You may not be able to leave right now.

You may feel trapped by fear, finances, children, immigration status, or church pressure.

You may feel voiceless or invisible.

But even here, God is with you.

You can begin taking small steps, inside yourself, to reclaim your dignity:

- Learn to recognize abusive patterns.

- Quietly gather important documents and resources, including your "go-bag." Ask a close friend or relative to keep it for you, if possible, in case you need to leave quickly.

- If you need to leave the home, do not tell him that you are leaving or give any indication of it. Leave in the middle of the night or while he is away from the house. It is one of the most dangerous times for a woman and children.

- Identify at least one safe person you can trust.

- Feed your spirit with God's truth, even in the midst of lies.

Remember: God is not asking you to stay in danger or submit to sin.

He is your refuge, your strength, and your advocate—even now.

"The Lord is close to the brokenhearted and saves those who are crushed in spirit." (Psalm 34:18)

You are not powerless.

And when you are ready, there is help, hope, and a way forward. The next chapter will give lists of resources so that you can begin your journey to safety and healing.

Conclusion: The God Who Makes All Things New

You are no longer defined by survival.

You are no longer trapped by the past.

You are a beloved, redeemed, and deeply loved daughter of God.

"Therefore, if anyone is in Christ, the new creation has come: The old has gone, the new is here!" (2 Corinthians 5:17)

God is not rushing you, and He is not finished with you. He promises to restore the years the locusts have eaten (Joel 2:25), to bring beauty from ashes (Isaiah 61:3), and to make all things new (Revelation 21:5).

You are part of His redemptive story.

You are no longer just surviving—you are stepping into a life rebuilt in Christ, clothed in His righteousness, held in His love, and called into His purpose.

This is not the end.

This is the beginning of something beautifully, eternally new.

Chapter 17 Discussion Questions

1. **Identity Reset**

   Which lie from your past still echoes the loudest ("You're worthless," "You failed," etc.)? What specific Scripture or truth about your identity in Christ most directly silences that lie?

2. **Whole-Person Healing**

   Spirit, soul, and body all bear trauma's marks differently. Where do you sense the greatest need for healing right now—spirit, soul, or body—and what first step might nurture that area this week?

3. **Healthy Boundaries & Holy Love**

   Think of one current relationship where you feel unsafe or drained. What boundary—large or small—could honor both your dignity and God's call to love in truth?

4. **Facing the Tension**

   Lysa TerKeurst says boundaries create "the tension of no longer cooperating with dysfunction." How does your heart or body react to that tension? What encouragement helps you hold the line?

5. **Finding Your Tribe**

   Isolation is a wound; safe connection is medicine. Which kind of support community (local group, online network, church ministry) most appeals to you right now, and what hesitations do you feel about stepping in?

6. **Rediscovering Joy**

   Recall one moment of unexpected joy or laughter since leaving (or while still inside) the abuse. What did that spark of joy tell you about God's heart for your future?

7. **Over-Functioning Detox**

   Where are you still carrying responsibilities that rightly belong to God or to others? What would "laying them down" look like in practical terms?

8. **Spiritual Practices for Renewal**

   Which practice has felt most life-giving in this season—prayer walks, journaling lament, Scripture meditation, worship music, silence? How could you carve consistent space for it?

9. **If You're Still in the Storm**

   List two "micro-acts" of resistance you can safely take right now (e.g., saving $10 a week, storing important documents, memorizing one grounding verse). How do these small steps nurture hope?

10. **Vision for the New**

    Picture your life five years from now, rebuilt on Christ rather than survival. What three words describe the atmosphere you long for in that future? What one decision today moves you a notch closer?

RESOURCES FOR WOMEN IN TOXIC RELATIONSHIPS

You Are Not Alone

As you close the final pages of this book, I want you to hear this clearly:

You do not have to walk the road ahead by yourself.

Whether you are still in the middle of crisis, just beginning to step into freedom, or already on the path of rebuilding your life, there are people, ministries, and communities ready to walk with you—people who understand what you've been through and are equipped to help you take your next steps with wisdom and courage.

You are part of a larger sisterhood of women who have walked through similar pain and survived. You are part of the family of God, where there are still safe, faithful people and places that reflect His heart.

This chapter offers a carefully selected list of trusted resources to help you as you move forward —from national helplines and Christian ministries to books, podcasts, and online communities where you can find truth, support, and practical help. This is by no means an exhaustive list but is a starting place of trustworthy resources, many of which have been a tremendous help to me and to others I have counseled.

You don't have to remember or use everything all at once.

Let this list simply be a toolbox you can return to when you need it, knowing that help is available, hope is real, and God is with you every step of the way.

National and Federal U.S. Resources

National Domestic Violence Hotline
24/7, confidential, multilingual support for victims and survivors of domestic violence
Phone: 800-799-7233 (SAFE)
Website: thehotline.org

National Sexual Assault Hotline (RAINN)
24/7 confidential support for survivors of sexual assault
Phone: 800-656-4673 (HOPE)
Website: rainn.org

National Human Trafficking Hotline

Support and referral services for victims of trafficking

Phone: 888-373-7888 or text "HELP" to 233733

Website: humantraffickinghotline.org

Domestic Shelters Directory

Search for safe housing and domestic violence services by zip code

Website: domesticshelters.org

Federal & Government Resources

WomensLaw.org (a project of the National Network to End Domestic Violence)

State-specific legal information, plain-language guides, help with restraining orders, and email hotline

Website: womenslaw.org

Office on Violence Against Women (OVW)

U.S. Department of Justice office offering information and grant support for survivors and providers

Website: justice.gov/ovw

National Coalition Against Domestic Violence (NCADV)

Advocacy, survivor stories, and national policy efforts

Website: ncadv.org

National Resource Center on Domestic Violence (NRCDV)

Research, policy, and training materials for advocates and survivors

Website: nrcdv.org

Futures Without Violence

Resources for survivors, advocates, healthcare workers, and faith communities

Website: futureswithoutviolence.org

Domestic Violence Legal Empowerment and Appeals Project.

https://www.dvleap.org/

State-Specific Legal Aid and Domestic Violence Coalitions

Every U.S. state has its own domestic violence coalition or network that can:

- Connect you to local shelters and legal aid
- Provide help with protection orders or custody concerns
- Offer advocacy and referrals

Search for your state's coalition here:

National Network to End Domestic Violence (NNEDV) Member Directory

Website: nnedv.org/content/state-u-s-territory-coalitions

Legal Advocacy and Protection Orders

Legal Aid Organizations (State-Based)

Many survivors qualify for free or low-cost legal representation; search through <u>womenslaw.org</u> or your state bar association.

Protection Orders / Restraining Orders

Each state has its own process — <u>womenslaw.org</u> provides detailed state-by-state guidance.

Court-Based Advocates / Domestic Violence Advocates

Many counties have specialized advocates who can help you navigate court processes, especially for restraining orders or custody concerns. Contact your local domestic violence program or court system for details.

Christian Ministries and Organizations

- **Psalm 82 Initiative** — <u>psalm82initiative.org</u>
- **Called to Peace Ministries (Joy Forrest)** — <u>calledtopeace.org</u>
- **Wilderness to Wild (Sarah McDugal)** — <u>wildernesstowild.com</u>
- **Helena Knowlton (Confusion to Clarity)** — <u>confusiontoclaritynow.com</u>
- **Andrew Bauman** — <u>andrewjbauman.com</u>

- **Gretchen Baskerville (The Life-Saving Divorce)** — lifesavingdivorce.com
- **Love Them To Life**—(Cherri Raws Freeman)— lovethemtolife.com
- **Leslie Vernick**—https://leslievernick.com
- **Chris Moles**—chrismoles.org (PeaceWorks University)
- **Tim Fletcher**—https://timfletcher.ca (healing from complex trauma and shame).

Christian Ministries that offer emotional support as well as some financial resources:

- **Give Her Wings**—giveherwings.com
- **Focus Ministries**— https://www.focusministries1.org/
- **Called To Peace Ministries**—calledtopeace.org

Recommended Books – this is not an exhaustive list but a good place to start

- *Boundaries* by Dr. Henry Cloud & Dr. John Townsend
- *Good Boundaries and Goodbyes* and *I Want to Trust You, But I Can't* by Lysa TerKeurst
- *The Life-Saving Divorce* by Gretchen Baskerville
- *Safe Church* by Andrew Bauman
- *Safe Churches* by Sarah McDugal
- *When the Church Harms God's People* by Diane Langberg
- *Is It Abuse?* by Darby Strickland
- *Is It Me?* by Natalie Hoffman

- *The Emotionally Destructive Marriage* by Leslie Vernick
- *How He Gets Into Her Head* by Don Hennessy
- *It's Not You* by Dr. Ramani Durvasula
- *Should I Stay or Should I Go?* by Dr. Ramani Durvasula
- *The Verbally Abusive Relationship* by Patricia Evans
- *Why Is He So Mean to Me?* by Cindy Burrell
- *Called to Peace* by Joy Forrest
- *Eyes Wide Open* by Dr. Debra Wingfield
- *Set Free: Finding Truth and Hope When a Loved One is Addicted* by Cherri Raws Freeman
- *When Narcissism Comes to Church* (and other books) by Chuck DeGroat
- *Something's Not Right* by Wade Mullen

Websites:

- *Flyingfreenow.com*—Natalie Hoffman—blog articles and links to her podcast.
- *Commandthecourtroom.com*—Attorney Wendy Hernandez. There is an interview with her on the Flying Free podcast episodes 220 and 329.
- *Lovethemtolife.com*—a resource for women who have loved ones in addiction.
- *Confusiontoclaritynow.com*—Helena Knowlton offers excellent articles on many topics regarding abusive relationships

- Calledtopeace.org—They provide "a compassionate, comprehensive, and Christ-centered response to those impacted by abuse."

Online Support Groups

You don't have to navigate healing alone—there are many online communities of Christian women walking through similar journeys. These groups offer encouragement, shared wisdom, and connection with others who truly understand.

Free Facebook Support Groups

- **Confusion to Clarity (Helena Knowlton)**
  facebook.com/groups/confusiontoclarity
- **The Life-Saving Divorce (Gretchen Baskerville)**
  facebook.com/groups/thelifesavingdivorce
- **Held and Healed (Heather Elizabeth)**
  facebook.com/groups/heldandhealed

Subscription-Based Support Groups

- **Arise (Helena Knowlton)**
  helenaknowlton.com/arise
- **Flying Free Kaleidoscope (Natalie Hoffman—for women who are not yet divorced)**
  flyingfreenow.com/join

- **Flying Higher (Natalie Hoffman—for women who are divorced)**
  flyingfreenow.com/join-flying-higher
- **Held and Healed (Heather Elizabeth—subscription community with expanded resources)**
  heldandhealed.com
- **Conquer (Leslie Vernick)**—leslievernick.com/conquer

Recommended Podcasts

These podcasts offer rich, compassionate, and biblically or therapeutically informed conversations for women healing from abuse, betrayal, addiction, and trauma.

- **The Flying Free Podcast**—Natalie Hoffman
  flyingfreenow.com/podcast
- **Therapy and Theology**—Lysa TerKeurst
  proverbs31.org/podcast
- **Bare Marriage Podcast**—Sheila Wray Gregoire
  baremarriage.com/podcast
- **Betrayal Trauma Recovery Podcast**—Anne Blythe
  btr.org/podcast
- **Surviving Narcissism Podcast**—Dr. Les Carter
  survivingnarcissism.tv/podcast
- **Navigating Narcissism Podcast**—Dr. Ramani Durvasula

podcasts.apple.com/us/podcast/navigating-narcissism-with-dr-ramani/id1613884517

As you explore these resources, remember this: **you are not alone, and you are not expected to walk this path by yourself.**

These books, podcasts, ministries, online groups, and professional services are here for you— not as burdens or obligations, but as lifelines, connections, and places where you can find support, wisdom, and hope.

You don't need to use every resource at once. You don't need to solve everything overnight. Healing is a journey, and you get to walk it one step at a time, with God's love guiding you.

The most important truth you carry is this: **you are deeply loved by your Creator, and He has never let you go.**

In the next (and final) chapter, we will bring this book to a close with a gentle, hopeful wrap-up —one that reminds you of who you are, where you've come from, and where God is leading you next.

Chapter 18 Discussion Questions

1. **Your First Lifeline**
   As you reviewed the resources in this chapter, was there one that immediately stood out or stirred hope in you? Why that one?

2. **Barriers to Reaching Out**
   What hesitations or fears rise up when you consider

joining a support group, talking to a counselor, or calling a helpline? What truth could gently counter those fears?

3. **Personalizing Your Toolbox**

   Imagine you are building a small "support toolkit" for your next step. Which 2–3 resources from this chapter would you include right now—and how might they serve your situation?

4. **Sifting the Noise**

   With so many resources listed, it's easy to feel overwhelmed. What would it look like to give yourself permission to start slowly and take in just what you need for today?

5. **Faith + Practical Help**

   Which resource blends both spiritual truth and practical support in a way that feels especially relevant to your healing?

6. **For the Woman Still in It**

   If you are still in the abusive relationship, what is *one safe, quiet step* you could take using something from this chapter? (It could be writing down a phone number, visiting a website, or saving a podcast.)

7. **Courage in Community**

   What do you hope a support community might offer you right now—encouragement, understanding, practical advice, spiritual grounding? What would it take to take one small step toward that?

8. **Paying It Forward (When You're Ready)**

   If you've already begun healing, is there a way you feel called to come alongside someone else—maybe by sharing a resource, a podcast, or even just your presence?

9. **Your Resource Map**

   Looking back over the entire list, are there categories you feel most drawn to—legal help, emotional support, spiritual teaching, practical steps? What does that say about where you are right now?

10. **Hope Is Not a Myth**

    Which part of this chapter (or the book as a whole) reminded you that hope is real—even if the road is long?

Chapter 19:

A FINAL WORD: YOU ARE NOT ALONE, AND THIS IS NOT THE END

A Pause to Breathe

Take a deep breath.

You have just walked through some of the most vulnerable, painful, and courageous topics a woman can face.

You have faced the truth about abuse, betrayal, addiction, trauma, and spiritual harm.

You have dared to ask hard questions—not just about your relationships, but about your faith, your identity, and your future.

And now, as you close this book, I want you to pause.

Breathe.

Look at how far you have already come.

You are brave.

You are strong.

You are dearly, unshakably loved by the God who created you.

Where You Have Come From

You are a survivor.

You have endured storms that many people will never understand.

You have wept, prayed, wrestled, and sometimes wondered if you would make it through.

But here you are.

Reading this.

Choosing to step into the light.

Choosing to seek truth, healing, and freedom.

Your past does not define you—but it has shaped you.

And God, the great Redeemer, knows how to take the broken pieces of your story and weave them into something beautiful and new.

Where You Are Now

You may not feel "healed."

You may not feel "whole."

You may still feel tired, uncertain, or scared.

That's okay.

Healing is not a straight line.

It is a layered, personal, sacred journey—and you are right where you need to be.

Give yourself grace.

Let yourself rest when you need to.

Take small steps when you're ready.

Lean into God's love, which holds you securely even on days when you feel weak.

You do not have to have it all figured out.

You are already deeply, fully, and perfectly loved.

Where God Is Leading You

God's heart for you has never changed.

He has been with you in the dark nights.

He has walked beside you in the moments of doubt.

And He is here now, inviting you forward—into a new chapter, a new season, a new sense of purpose and belonging.

There is still joy ahead.

There are still safe, life-giving relationships ahead.

There is still healing ahead—not because you can earn it, but because God delights in restoring His daughters.

Dream again.

Pray again.

Let your heart open, even just a little, to the possibility that the best is not behind you—it is ahead.

One More Story

This story is from a precious friend who is in Heaven now, spending the rest of eternity with the One whom she loved so dearly. She gave me this writing many years ago when I was going through a very dark time myself. I believe she would want you to hear her heart.

Journeying

"How did you get from the broken person you were to the person you are now?'

My friend surprised me with her question. I thought back over the years and tried to answer it accurately, reasonably. I realize my answer is one that millions of people can duplicate... now, and down through the centuries of time...

There was...I remember...

Forcing toast down day after day while being wracked with uncontrollable sobs

Nightmares, consuming nightmares

Constant diarrhea...digestive upheavals

Church...a hymn, the familiar beloved Scriptures would send me into a deluge of tears.

Hanging onto myself to restrain the urge to jump in front of an oncoming train.

People who said...'You remind me of a dog on its back, paws in the air, in the middle of the street, crying: 'Please, someone, hit me again."

I remember crying to God...

This isn't how it's supposed to be, Lord.

I lived for You. I dedicated my life to you, each day to You.

I gave all for You, for Your cause.

I lived by Your precepts, walked in Your way.

All the things I believed...was taught as a child, staked my life on...

Where are they?

This isn't how it's supposed to be, Lord.

In my sobbing, through my tears, my shattered dreams, I said to Him:

'Lord, no, don't rebuild my faith.

Rather, build my faith Your way.

Tell me that You love me and build my Faith Your way.'

I believe He has done this. How?

> 1. Prayer – talking to Him, focusing my mind, my thoughts was difficult, impossible. I decided to write to Him, words on paper, not in the air. I could focus better. I got a notebook. I wrote to the Lord each day. I told Him where I was inside, what I thought, how I felt, my worries, my perplexities, my fears, my disappointments, my pain, begged for His help. He heard it all in detail, each day...He still does.
>
> 2. I thought of myself as taking a journey, like Abram of the Old Testament...leaving the familiar, the life he knew, and setting out to follow God. He didn't know where that journey would lead him, but he believed God, and he followed Him.
>
> For myself, I had lost everything I held dear, everything I had staked my life on. I had nowhere to turn, except to God. I did that and believed He would lead me. I had

*no choice but to follow Him, and like Abram of old, I too
set out on a journey with God, into strange territory,
with no inkling where that would lead me.*

*3. I was pretty old...almost sixty. I needed money to live
on. What could I do at that age?*

*A friend invited me to join her taking a crash course in
real estate sales. 'No, I wasn't interested. No way would
I ever do that.'*

*'Just think about it. The course starts in two weeks.
What could you lose?'*

*When I look back, I see God's hand...whew, do I ever see
it clearly. I tried to find another idea to earn money, but
I lived on a remote resort island, barren in the winter...
so I joined my friend in the course in real estate sales...
and I absolutely loved it.*

I got a chance to use abilities I never knew I had.

I honed and sharpened other abilities.

*I was thrust into a totally secular world...I had spent
my life in the religious world.*

I learned to swim with the sharks and survive...and succeed.

**Suddenly there was money to live on, to afford clothes,
music, books, a car, a place to live...I, who never before
understood what a mortgage was.**

*I was affirmed, endorsed, respected. Gradually my self-
image grew healthy again.*

*I saw the verse in the Psalms about 'being fearfully and
wonderfully made' as a reality, and I fell to my knees in
awe of my Creator.*

4. I lived in the Psalms.

I never understood them before...not really. Suddenly they came alive. They were where I was...the cries for help, the heartache, the tears, the hope, the praise, the joy, the sorrow. I'm still there...I'm there every morning. They are beautiful, blessed, precious.

5. I had a few good friends...just as many as God knew I needed...and they showed up just when He knew I needed them. *Then there were new friends, and renewed old dear friendships, friends I hadn't heard from for years. My, I learned what a beautiful, priceless treasure a friend is.*

6. When you come to the end of yourself, and with nowhere else to turn, decide to set out on a journey with just you and God. *It's both humbling and awesome each day... and there are these special surprises around corners... One morning I shall never forget, I was overcome with sobs. Alone, by the window, in the silence, a little bird began to sing just outside.*

I interpreted his cheery song as saying, 'God loves you. I'm here to tell you that...here's my song, just for you.'

You find your needs met unexpectedly. Time and again when I had a question, a perplexity, a decision, a problem, the answers would come in all kinds of ways...a conversation, a phone call, a TV program, a newspaper article, a book, the Scriptures. I learned God has no limit on the media He uses.

The years have passed. The Psalmist says:

'God is close to the brokenhearted...' (Psalm 34:18).
'He heals the brokenhearted and binds up their wounds'
(Psalm 147:3)

I believe...I know...He has done that for me.
I live in peace, a beautiful deep peace.
The nightmares are gone.
Toast is enjoyed...no longer forced down in sobs.
Trains no longer lure me to jump in front of them.

I am still on my journey with God...a no nonsense,
practical reality.
He and I just 'are.'
I simply walk with Him, enjoying Him, learning to
love Him, this beautiful world He has made, and the
people in it.
I know now that God is love, and that He loves me.
Yes, He is the very core of my existence.

I've wanted to write about this for a long time, about
my precious Lord.
It's been hard to find the words to capture these years
on paper.

I invite you to set out on your won journey with God.
You'll love it, you'll be delighted, surprised, excited,
overwhelmed.

He's waiting for you...
As He waited so long, so very long, for me."

A Final Blessing

Beloved sister,

May you know—deep in your soul—that you are seen, known, and loved by the God who created you.

May His Spirit comfort you when you feel alone, strengthen you when you feel weak, and rejoice over you as you take each brave step forward.

May you walk in the truth of who you are:

Redeemed.

Restored.

Set free.

Held forever in the arms of Jesus.

"The Lord your God is with you, the Mighty Warrior who saves. He will take great delight in you; in His love He will no longer rebuke you, but will rejoice over you with singing." (Zephaniah 3:17)

You are not alone.

And this is not the end.

This is the beginning of a new, beautiful, redeemed chapter—written by the One who loves you beyond measure.

Chapter 19 Final Reflection Questions

1. **A Breath of Recognition**

    As you pause at the end of this journey, what are you most surprised to realize about how far you've come?

2. **The Voice You Carry Forward**

    What harsh or painful message once defined you that you are now ready to lay down? What truth from God's heart will you carry in its place?

3. **Your Journey with God**

    In the story "Journeying," the writer asked God not to rebuild her old faith, but to build it *His way*. What part of that prayer resonates with your own experience?

4. **Sacred Surprises**

    Have you had any moments—big or small—when you sensed God meeting you unexpectedly, like the little bird in the story? What did it speak to your heart?

5. **The Psalms and Your Healing**

    The story describes how the Psalms came alive as she healed. Is there a particular Scripture or verse that has anchored you through this season?

6. **Dreaming Again**

    What dream, hope, or possibility is beginning to stir again in your heart—even if it still feels fragile or far away?

7. **Companions for the Road**

    Who are the "few good friends" or safe people who

have walked beside you in this season? How has their presence reflected God's love?

8. **This Isn't the End**

   What are you sensing God inviting you into now—not in pressure, but in gentle love? What new beginning is quietly unfolding?

9. **What You Want to Remember**

   Of all the truths, stories, and Scriptures in this book, what is the one thing you most want to remember in your next chapter?

10. **If You Were to Write a Letter to the Next Woman**

    What simple words of hope or truth would you share with another woman just beginning her healing journey?

A NOTE TO MINISTRY LEADERS:

One of the great challenges in walking with women in destructive relationships is that many never say a word. Especially in Christian communities—where a husband's sobriety is often viewed as a spiritual victory—his wife may feel pressure to stay silent about ongoing control, emotional harm, or coercion.

This checklist is offered to pastors, women's ministry leaders, counselors, and trusted mentors who want to recognize signs of hidden abuse and respond with wisdom and care. It is not meant to label or diagnose. but to help discern when a woman may need a safe space, gentle support, and time to name what's really going on.

Recognizing Hidden Abuse in the Church

Checklist for Identifying Potential Abuse in Women Married to Men in Addiction Recovery

Abuse often hides in plain sight—especially when the husband has achieved sobriety and is publicly celebrated for his "testimony." This checklist is intended for pastors, ministry leaders, counselors, and women's ministry teams to help identify women who may be suffering in silence. It is not a diagnostic tool but a guide for discernment, compassion, and proactive care.

Emotional and Behavioral Indicators

- Appears anxious, tense, or overly cautious around her husband.
- Downplays her own needs, opinions, or feelings in conversations.
- Frequently blames herself for marital issues or spiritual "failures."
- Shows signs of confusion, chronic self-doubt, or spiritual guilt.
- Is noticeably different (more quiet, nervous, or withdrawn) in her husband's presence.
- Says things like, "He's not drinking anymore, so I should be grateful," even when describing dysfunction.
- Uses spiritual language to excuse mistreatment (e.g., "God is refining me," "I need to submit better").
- Avoids discussing her marriage or redirects when asked.

Relational and Social Patterns

- Gradually withdraws from women's groups, church events, or social connections.
- Rarely attends church without her husband.
- Frequently checks in with her husband before committing to plans or answering questions.
- Hesitates to accept help or invitations, citing her husband's preferences.
- Avoids overnight retreats or events requiring time away.
- Children appear unusually quiet, anxious, or overly obedient.

Spiritual and Theological Red Flags

- Expresses pressure to be a "godly wife" at all costs, regardless of harm.
- Quotes Scripture in a way that reinforces her silence or suffering.
- Frames her husband's harmful behavior as part of his sanctification or testimony.
- Indicates fear that boundary-setting would dishonor God.
- Believes abuse is not present because her husband is sober.

Controlling or Manipulative Behavior by the Husband

- Frequently speaks for her or corrects her—even in casual settings.
- Appears spiritual in public but resists accountability or counsel.
- Controls how their marriage is portrayed to others.
- Minimizes or mocks her in front of others.
- Holds visible positions in church leadership while lacking genuine humility.

Indirect or Situational Clues

- Mentions not having access to money or major household decisions.
- Jokes about "walking on eggshells" at home.
- Exhibits signs of physical stress: fatigue, weight changes, illness, or chronic anxiety.
- Is fearful of saying or doing the "wrong thing."
- Rejects offers of support, saying "It's not that bad," or "He's changed a lot."

If Several Indicators Are Present:

- Do not confront her directly about abuse unless she opens the door.
- Offer a safe, nonjudgmental presence. Build trust slowly and consistently.
- Ask gentle, open-ended questions:

  - "Are you feeling safe and supported at home?"
  - "Do you feel like you have a voice in your marriage?"
  - "Would it be helpful to talk with someone privately?"

- Connect her with trained counselors, women's advocates, or support ministries if she expresses concern or interest.
- Continue to pursue her with grace, truth, and patience. Many women in coercive relationships have been spiritually conditioned to remain silent.

About the Author

Cherri Raws Freeman grew up at America's Keswick, a Christian conference and addiction recovery center founded by her great-grandfather. With deep roots in ministry and a passion for walking alongside the hurting, Cherri has dedicated her life to helping others find hope and healing in Christ.

She holds a B.S. in Biology from Wheaton College and worked for many years in both the medical field and science education. She is a certified Life Coach, a Board-Certified Master Mental Health Coach, a certified Abuse Advocate, and a certified Exchanged Life Counselor and Addiction Recovery Coach through Grace Fellowship International.

In 2013, Cherri founded *Love Them to Life*, a ministry offering help and hope to those with addicted loved ones—born out of her personal journey as a mother of two children in addiction. She is also the author of *Beside Still Waters: Discovering Peace in the Midst of Your Child's Addiction* and *Set Free: Finding Truth and Hope When a Loved One is Addicted.*

Her most recent work flows from her experience in a destructive marriage that opened her eyes to the often-overlooked intersection of addiction and abuse. Cherri now counsels and coaches through Grace Fellowship International and continues to support women through *Love Them to Life,* including a free online weekly support group for women who have loved ones in addiction. Cherri is also available to speak to churches and groups.

You can learn more or get in touch at www.lovethemtolife.com or email lovethemtolife@gmail.com.

Author's Note

The stories and experiences shared in this book are told from my personal perspective and those of the women who have shared their stories. Some names, timelines, and identifying details have been changed to protect privacy. While I speak honestly about my lived experience and that of other brave women, the intent is not to accuse or defame anyone but to bring healing and clarity to those who may be walking through similar circumstances.

Acknowledgements

To name every person who has impacted my journey and healing from abuse would be impossible—but there are some I must thank for surrounding me with love and strength when I needed it most.

Dianne, Donna, Beth, and Kris—your friendship has been a steady anchor through the wild storms of life. You have encouraged me in ways you may never fully realize. Katy, your example of perseverance despite incredible hardship and your deep love for Jesus constantly inspire me. I am so grateful for all my friends who are Warrior-Daughters of the Most High.

To my wonderful children—Sara, Chris, Gloria, Susy, and Ali—you stepped in and said, "No more." You helped me escape a nightmare, and I will always be grateful for your courage and love. Being your mom and now Grammie is the greatest privilege of my life and I love you all so deeply.

To my niece Jenny, who opened her home to me for far longer than either of us expected—thank you. Your generosity became a refuge.

To my "brother" Bill—thank you for standing by me, even when it was hard and uncomfortable. Your loyalty has meant the world.

To John Woodward and the staff at Grace Fellowship International—thank you for all you've done to support my healing.

To those who didn't believe me when I said the last book would be the final one—thank you for recognizing the need for this one. You gently nudged me out of my comfort zone, and I'm better for it.

To the brave women who entrusted me with your stories—what you have endured is not in vain. Your voices matter, and your pain has purpose.

To my friends, family, and clients who have read and reread the many iterations of the book and patiently made suggestions and edits along the way, I appreciate you more than I can say.

And most of all, thank you, Jesus, for rescuing me and setting my feet on solid ground.

Soli Deo Gloria.

A Note on the Writing Process

Throughout the writing of this book, I used ChatGPT as a collaborative tool to support and refine the creative process. Every idea, theme, and direction came from my own experience, prayer, and conviction. The AI helped me research themes, clarify thoughts, organize material, and polish my voice—but the heart, theology, and lived reality behind these pages are entirely my own.

I share this as part of my commitment to transparency and integrity. Just as an author might work with an editor or writing coach, I've used this tool ethically and intentionally, with full creative ownership of the work.

Endnotes

i   Gabor Maté, "Beyond Drugs: The Universal Experience of Addiction," drgabormate.com, accessed May 26, 2025, https://drgabormate.com/wp-content/uploads/2017/04/Beyond-Drugs.pdf

ii   Marcus Warner, *Understanding the Wounded Heart* (*Deeper Walk International*, 2019).

iii   Dr. Debra Wingfield, House of Peace Publications, houseofpeacepubs.com

iv   Ibid.

v   Ibid.

vi   Lisa Aronson Fontes, "Abuse Cannot Be Blamed on Alcoholism or Mental Illness," Psychology Today, 2015.

vii   Jerold J. Kreisman and Hal Straus, *I Hate You—Don't Leave Me: Understanding the Borderline Personality* (Avon Books, 1991).

viii   Chuck DeGroat, *When Narcissism Comes to Church: Healing Your Community from Emotional and Spiritual Abuse* (InterVarsity Press, 2020).

ix   Leslie Vernick, *The Emotionally Destructive Relationship*, quoted on Goodreads. https://www.goodreads.com/work/quotes/988215-the-emotionally-destructive-relationship

x   Sheila Wray Gregoire, *The Great Sex Rescue: The Lies You've Been Taught and How to Recover What God Intended* (Baker Books, 2021).

xi   Andrew Bauman, *Safe Church* (Baker Books, 2025) p 84.

xii   Natalie Hoffman, *Is It Me? Making Sense of Your Confusing Marriage: A Christian Woman's Guide to Hidden Emotional and Spiritual Abuse* (Flying Free, 2019).

xiii   Sheila Wray Gregoire, *The Great Sex Rescue: The Lies You've Been Taught and How to Recover What God Intended* (Baker Books, 2021).

xiv   Gretchen Baskerville, *The Life-Saving Divorce: Hope for People Leaving Destructive Relationships* (Life-Saving Press, 2020).

xv   Sarah McDugal, Wilderness to Wild.com writings on coercive control and abuse in Christian marriages.

xvi   Gretchen Baskerville, *The Life-Saving Divorce: Hope for People Leaving Destructive Relationships* (Life-Saving Press, 2020).

xvii   As *Long As He Needs Me*" from *Oliver!*, lyrics by Lionel Bart. © 1960 Essex Music Ltd. Originally performed by Georgia Brown (West End) and Shani Wallis (1968 film adaptation).

xviii   Lysa Terkeurst, *Good Boundaries and Goodbyes* (Nelson Books, 2022) p. 86

xix   https://spiritualsoundingboard.com/2019/10/07/pastor-neil-schori-urges-pastors-and-church-leaders-to-get-it-right-about-domestic-violence/.

xx   https://theallendercenter.org/2025/05/how-to-guard-against-sexism-and-abuse-in-christian-communities-with-dr-andrew-j-bauman/

xxi   Wade Mullen, "Responding Well to a Scandal," *Uncommon Pursuit*, December 15, 2023, https://up.uncommonpursuit.net/t/responding-well-to-a-scandal-wade-mullens/3358

xxii   Glenn Patrick Doyle, X (formerly Twitter) post, March 5, 2024, x.com/drdoylesays

xxiii   Mowczko, Marg. "Kephalē and 'Male Headship' in Paul's Letters." *Marg Mowczko*, https://margmowczko.com/kephale-and-male-headship-in-pauls-letters/

xxiv   Mowczko, Marg. "Submission in Christian Marriage." Marg Mowczko, https://margmowczko.com/submission-in-marriage/

xxv   Mowczko, Marg. "Kephalē ('head') as Metaphor in First-Century Texts." Marg Mowczko, https://margmowczko.com/kephale-head-philo-first-century/

xxvi   https://news.illinoisstate.edu/2012/10/out-of-the-drew-peterson-spotlight-alum-fights-domestic-violence/.